Start Investing in REITs

Start Investing in REITs

Build a real estate portfolio without buying a single property

Adrian Lorne

Mindful Pages

Published in 2025

ISBN: 9789371776929 (PB)
ISBN: 9789371774420 (eBook)

Published by

Mindful Pages
Imprint of Alpha Editions LLC
312 W. 2nd St #1834
Casper, WY 82601, USA

Content

Introduction
The Real Estate Revolution You Can't See

Real estate has long been celebrated as a cornerstone of wealth—a marker of stability, accomplishment, and financial maturity. Owning a home, perhaps even a family estate, has come to signify economic success in the public imagination. Yet, beneath this comforting narrative lies a subtle but pervasive misconception, one that often ensnares individuals in cycles of debt, maintenance headaches, and illiquidity. This book challenges that convention, revealing a modern evolution in property ownership—an approach that allows you to participate in real estate wealth without ever signing a deed or patching a leaking roof.

Start Investing in REITs offers a fresh lens: property ownership decoupled from the physical asset itself. Through Real Estate Investment Trusts, or REITs, investors gain access to real estate's income potential and diversification benefits without confronting the operational burdens of traditional ownership. This is not merely a manual on financial instruments; it is a reimagining of what it means to engage with real estate in the 21st century. The implications extend far beyond returns, touching on philosophical, economic, and behavioural dimensions.

Why has real estate investment remained so closely tied to tangible property for so long? Partly, the answer lies in culture, partly in psychology, and partly in the institutional frameworks that have shaped markets over generations. Homeownership is more than shelter—it embodies security, identity, and legacy. Yet these emotional anchors often obscure reality: decades-long mortgages, ongoing responsibilities, and risks capable of destabilising financial stability. Many investors discover, too late, that the very homes they considered assets can feel more like burdens than wealth.

The traditional model of property-based wealth relies heavily on debt, with mortgages functioning as double-edged swords. Leverage can magnify returns—but it equally magnifies vulnerability. The so-called 'mortgage-industrial complex' encourages long-term indebtedness, frequently placing the symbolism of ownership above liquidity and genuine financial autonomy. The illusion of control, often touted as a benefit, becomes fragile when markets decline, maintenance crises arise, or legal issues intervene. In such moments, ownership can reveal itself as a trap masquerading as security.

This book shifts the conversation from bricks and mortar to cash flow and yield. Real estate, in this view, is a dynamic asset class to be assessed for its income-generating potential rather than square footage. This mindset liberates investors from the physical anchors of property, opening avenues for diversification, scale, and accessibility. REITs form the linchpin of this approach, marrying the stability of real estate with the liquidity and transparency of public markets.

Understanding REITs demands more than technical knowledge; it requires context. Originating from legislative efforts to democratise access to real estate income, REITs dismantled barriers that had confined property investment to a privileged few. They provide structures designed to deliver reliable dividends through mandated income distributions, governed by strict transparency and regulatory oversight. This combination of yield and trust distinguishes REITs from other asset classes, positioning them as uniquely accessible channels to real estate participation.

REITs also exemplify the broader evolution of ownership—from physical possession to financial and digital representation. Just as industries have been reshaped by virtualisation, real estate investment has embraced liquidity and scale once unimaginable. Investors no longer contend with tenant disputes or complex property laws; instead, they engage with a streamlined, systematised, and largely automated process.

The appeal extends beyond convenience. REITs span diverse sectors—from retail and healthcare to data centres and green infrastructure—allowing investors to balance stability with growth potential. Whether the objective is steady income or exposure to emerging niches, REITs provide versatile tools for portfolio construction.

Yet this book does not ignore risk or misunderstanding. It clarifies distinctions between public and private REITs, highlighting trade-offs in transparency versus exclusivity. It examines cognitive biases and emotional pitfalls that can impair traditional property investment, illustrating how REITs encourage discipline through structure. It addresses macroeconomic influences—interest rates, market volatility, taxation—equipping readers with frameworks to navigate complexity confidently.

At its core, this is a book about freedom: freedom from the physical, financial, and emotional encumbrances of traditional ownership. It invites a redefinition of wealth—not as possession of things, but as mastery over systems that generate income and growth. Through REITs, investors gain stakes in infrastructure supporting communities and economies worldwide—from hospitals and malls to logistics hubs and data centres—without ever setting foot on the properties themselves.

Readers are encouraged to challenge assumptions and adopt mental models informed by behavioural finance and real-world evidence. This book aims to educate and empower, fostering a philosophy of real estate investment that honours income, control, and diversification, while safeguarding time and peace of mind.

Start Investing in REITs promises that building a meaningful, resilient property portfolio no longer requires the burdens of physical ownership. It offers entry into a quieter revolution—one unseen, yet capable of profoundly reshaping your financial future. Here is your invitation to join that shift and redefine what it means to participate in real estate today.

Chapter 1
Why We Still Worship the House

The cultural reverence for homeownership runs deep, woven into society as a near-sacred rite of passage. Owning a property is often framed as the ultimate marker of financial success—a tangible emblem of security, stability, and accomplishment. Yet beneath this veneration lies a complex interplay of psychological and social forces that tether individuals to the myth of the "safe" roof: the notion that possession equates to control, protection, and lasting value. This chapter unravels those emotional attachments, exploring how ideas of security, legacy, and pride become entwined with bricks and mortar, subtly shaping behaviour and influencing financial choices.

The perception that a house provides shelter extends far beyond its physical walls. It occupies a symbolic space as a sanctuary from uncertainty, amplified over generations through social conditioning. Owning a home is often seen as an investment in the future—an inheritance for children, a foundation for identity and belonging. These unspoken psychological needs—security, pride, continuity—exert a powerful gravitational pull, which helps explain why renting or investing in abstract financial instruments often feels less tangible, and therefore less appealing.

Yet the emotional valuation of homeownership frequently obscures the practical realities. The romanticised notion of "owning your castle" glosses over the fact that most buyers enter the market deeply indebted. Mortgages, often celebrated as stepping stones to wealth, operate primarily as long-term liabilities. One might call this debt as destiny: a structural system in which homeownership becomes synonymous with decades of repayment obligations, often at the cost of liquidity and financial flexibility. Far from a straightforward route to wealth, the combination of interest payments, upkeep, property taxes, and market volatility can erode both value and freedom.

This entrenched model is reinforced by what might be termed the mortgage-industrial complex—a confluence of financial institutions, regulatory frameworks, and cultural narratives that collectively encourage debt accumulation over genuine asset growth. The economic architecture incentivises borrowing to acquire property rather than investing in more liquid, income-generating assets. Consequently, homeowners often find themselves tied to a singular, illiquid asset requiring constant attention and expense. The dream of financial independence through property can too easily be replaced by the reality of perpetual indebtedness and constrained capital.

Complicating matters further is the illusion of control commonly attributed to ownership. The idea that possessing a home confers autonomy is pervasive, yet in practice, that control is partial and precarious. Markets can swing, legal entanglements—whether zoning disputes or tenant issues—can arise, and deferred maintenance can escalate into crises. Homeownership, rather than offering liberation, can expose individuals to risks and obligations that undermine wealth and well-being alike. The paradox is clear: possession can become entrapment.

Against this backdrop, it is vital to reconsider the premises of real estate investment. Rather than seeing property as a static object defined by location or size, investors are encouraged to view it as a cash flow-generating asset class. The emphasis shifts from square footage to yield, from the physical structure to the income it produces. This reframing compels critical thinking about capital deployment and financial goals, and it opens the door to alternative investment models, such as Real Estate Investment Trusts (REITs), which separate the benefits of property wealth from the burdens of physical management.

This chapter sets the stage for a fundamental shift in mindset. It challenges longstanding assumptions about ownership, offering a more nuanced understanding of real estate's role in personal finance. By examining the cultural, psychological, and economic forces underpinning the homeownership ideal, readers are encouraged to look beyond the veneer of safety and status toward the structural realities that truly shape wealth creation. The discussion is practical, grounded in the realities of contemporary markets, and aimed at helping investors make strategic, informed decisions about building a portfolio that aligns with both present conditions and future aspirations.

Through illustrative examples, the chapter highlights the tangible and intangible costs of conventional homeownership—financial, emotional, and operational—contrasting them with the opportunities afforded by income-focused approaches. It provides a framework for understanding why so many remain wedded to property, despite its limitations, and how a cash flow-oriented perspective can offer greater freedom and resilience. True control and security, the argument goes, stem not from holding keys but from mastering the income streams that underlie property value.

By the chapter's conclusion, readers should emerge with a clearer perspective on the myths surrounding homeownership, the economic trade-offs it conceals, and the strategic advantages of treating real estate as an income-generating asset class. This foundation primes investors to engage critically with REITs and to reconceive wealth in terms of financial freedom rather than physical possession—setting the stage for a form of real estate investment that liberates rather than confines, and that prizes yield over square footage.

The Myth of the 'Safe' Roof

Few symbols in modern society carry as much emotional and cultural weight as the notion of home ownership. It is widely accepted as the hallmark of adulthood, the ultimate achievement on the path to financial maturity. The phrase "safe roof over your head" evokes a sense of comfort, permanence, and refuge from the unpredictable forces of life. Yet, this seemingly self-evident truth—that owning a home is synonymous with security—deserves closer scrutiny. Beneath its reassuring veneer lies a complex psychological narrative shaped by deep-seated human needs, cultural reinforcement, and economic incentives. The idea of the 'safe' roof is less a universal reality and more a powerful social construct that shapes behaviour and influences financial decision-making in profound ways.

At the heart of this myth is the emotional architecture of security. Humans instinctively seek shelter as a means of survival and stability, and the home serves as the physical embodiment of that quest. But this instinct extends beyond mere protection from the elements; it encompasses the desire for a stable identity and a controlled environment amid a chaotic world. The home becomes a psychological anchor, a place where individuals and families assert their place in society and the continuity of their lineage. This association between home and safety is not only primal but culturally amplified, particularly in societies where land and property ownership have historically signified status and permanence. This cultural narrative positions the house as an unassailable fortress—one that promises not just shelter but a form of existential certainty.

However, the security promised by home ownership is not absolute; it is mediated by unspoken psychological needs that complicate the relationship between people and property. The desire for legacy plays a significant role. Owning property is often perceived as a means of creating an inheritance, a tangible asset to be passed down through generations. This intergenerational transfer of wealth fosters a sense of pride and accomplishment that transcends the immediate financial implications of ownership. Such pride is intertwined with notions of autonomy and control, feeding the belief that ownership grants mastery over one's environment and future. Yet, these intangible benefits can obscure the tangible costs and vulnerabilities embedded in the very fabric of homeownership.

Consider the psychological phenomenon known as the 'endowment effect,' wherein individuals assign greater value to possessions simply because they own them. This bias reinforces the emotional attachment to one's home, sometimes blinding owners to objective assessments of financial prudence. For many, the home ceases to be just an asset; it becomes an extension of the self, making the prospect of selling or diversifying investment strategies psychologically fraught. This attachment can hinder rational financial decisions, locking individuals into illiquid, high-maintenance investments that may not serve their long-term goals.

Real-world examples illustrate the paradox of the 'safe' roof. The 2008 global financial crisis starkly exposed how the perception of homeownership as an invulnerable bastion of wealth was fundamentally flawed. Millions faced foreclosure, plummeting property values, and shattered financial security, revealing how homes, far from being safe harbours, are subject to market volatility, systemic risk, and regulatory failures. This reality clashes with the deeply ingrained belief that owning property is a surefire safeguard against economic uncertainty. Yet, even in less extreme conditions, homeowners routinely encounter maintenance emergencies, legal disputes, and fluctuating property taxes—realities that complicate the idealised narrative of control and safety.

Cultural reinforcement also plays a critical role in sustaining the myth. Media, education systems, and financial institutions propagate the message that buying a home is not just an economic choice but a social imperative. Advertisements celebrate the emotional fulfilment of homeownership, while governments often incentivise property purchase through tax benefits and subsidies, reinforcing its primacy as a vehicle for wealth accumulation. This creates a feedback loop in which the aspiration for a 'safe' roof becomes entwined with social status and identity, marginalising alternative investment strategies and perspectives.

The interplay of these psychological and cultural forces produces a powerful incentive to conform, even when alternative paths might offer superior financial outcomes. For many, the appeal of owning a tangible asset—something they can see, touch, and personalise—outweighs the advantages of more abstract investment vehicles that generate income without physical custody. This preference is further compounded by the cognitive comfort derived from familiarity and tradition, which often trumps analytical evaluation of risks and rewards. As a result, millions remain committed to an asset class that, while emotionally satisfying, may impose significant financial constraints.

Understanding the myth of the 'safe' roof requires a multidisciplinary perspective, drawing from behavioural finance, sociology, and economic history. It invites a critical examination of how deeply held beliefs shape financial behaviour and how these beliefs interact with structural market realities. The reverence for homeownership is not merely a matter of individual preference but a product of collective narratives that have evolved over centuries. By unpacking these layers, investors and readers alike can begin to distinguish between the emotional allure of property and its practical implications as an asset.

This insight has profound implications for how we think about real estate as a component of personal wealth. If homeownership is often motivated by psychological and social needs as much as by financial logic, then the challenge becomes how to reconcile these dimensions with the demands of effective investment strategy. The path forward involves recognising that security and legacy can be achieved through means that do not require physical possession or the burdens it entails. In this context, the emergence of income-producing investment vehicles, such as Real Estate Investment Trusts (REITs), offers a compelling alternative that aligns emotional aspirations with financial pragmatism.

REITs, by decoupling ownership from physical management, provide a new framework for experiencing the benefits traditionally associated with owning a home—stable income, potential appreciation, and a sense of participation in community infrastructure—without the liabilities that have long been accepted as unavoidable. This model challenges the centrality of the 'safe' roof by presenting real estate as a dynamic income-generating asset, accessible, diversified, and manageable within a broader portfolio. In doing so, it addresses the very psychological needs that underpin the myth, reframing security and legacy in terms of cash flow rather than square footage.

Ultimately, deconstructing the myth of the 'safe' roof is an invitation to question inherited assumptions about wealth and ownership. It encourages a shift from identity-based investing towards a more detached, analytical, and opportunity-focused approach. By understanding the emotional and cultural underpinnings of why homeownership is so revered, readers can better navigate their own relationship with real estate and make choices that serve their financial goals more effectively. The path to true security, it turns out, may lie not in the walls that surround us but in the streams of income those walls can generate.

Debt as Destiny

The act of purchasing a home is often heralded as a cornerstone of financial success—a tangible step toward wealth accumulation and stability. Yet, this widely accepted milestone conceals a more complex reality: for the vast majority of homeowners, real estate investment begins not with capital accumulation, but with debt. The mortgage, a seemingly necessary instrument to bridge aspiration and affordability, becomes the defining feature of homeownership. This chapter explores the insidious nature of what might be termed the "mortgage-industrial complex," a pervasive system that prioritises debt servicing above liquidity or financial freedom. By examining the structural, cultural, and economic factors that have entrenched debt as destiny in property investment, we reveal the true costs and limitations of conventional homeownership.

At its core, the mortgage is a financial mechanism designed to enable purchase today in exchange for a long-term commitment to repay principal plus interest. While this arrangement opens the door to property ownership for many, it simultaneously binds them to decades of fixed obligations. The average mortgage term—typically 25 to 30 years—is a substantial portion of an individual's working life, during which income must be continually allocated to service this debt. This commitment significantly reduces financial flexibility, constrains savings potential, and exposes homeowners to interest rate risks and market fluctuations. Far from being a simple step on the road to wealth, the mortgage often functions as a persistent financial burden that colours every subsequent decision.

The term "mortgage-industrial complex" encapsulates the multifaceted network of banks, lenders, insurers, government policies, and cultural norms that collectively sustain and promote this debt-first investment model. Financial institutions generate enormous revenue from mortgage interest payments, fees, and ancillary services, creating powerful incentives to maintain and expand mortgage lending. Meanwhile, governments frequently subsidise home buying through tax incentives, guarantees, and regulatory frameworks that encourage borrowing over saving. Together, these forces create a self-reinforcing system where homeownership is tied inextricably to indebtedness, often at the expense of liquidity and investment diversification.

One critical but overlooked consequence of this system is the illusion of ownership it fosters. While homeowners hold legal title to their property, the reality is that a significant portion of the home's value is financed through debt. Until the mortgage is fully repaid—which may take decades—owners possess limited equity and remain beholden to lenders. This precarious position exposes individuals to risks such as foreclosure in cases of income disruption or adverse economic conditions. The financial stress associated with mortgage debt has measurable effects on mental health and life satisfaction, illustrating that ownership underpinned by heavy debt is not synonymous with security.

The cultural narrative surrounding mortgages often frames them as a positive form of leverage—a tool that accelerates wealth building by allowing individuals to control valuable assets without upfront capital. While leverage can amplify returns, it also magnifies losses and risk exposure. The global financial crisis of 2008 stands as a stark testament to the dangers of overleveraging in real estate. Millions of homeowners found themselves underwater, owing more on their mortgages than their homes were worth, with devastating personal and societal consequences. This event highlighted how mortgage debt, far from being a benign facilitator of homeownership, can become a catalyst for widespread financial instability.

Moreover, the mortgage-industrial complex shapes consumer behaviour in subtle but significant ways. The availability of credit encourages purchasing decisions driven more by borrowing capacity than by financial prudence or strategic investment goals. This phenomenon inflates property prices, contributing to housing bubbles and affordability crises in many markets worldwide. It also fosters an attachment to a single, illiquid asset, limiting investors' ability to diversify their portfolios or respond flexibly to changing economic circumstances. The mortgage effectively ties up capital in an asset that is costly to maintain and slow to convert to cash, restricting overall financial agility.

Critically, this system disproportionately affects younger generations and those with less initial capital. As property prices escalate, entry barriers rise, compelling prospective buyers to take on ever larger debts. This cycle can delay wealth accumulation and homeownership milestones, exacerbating intergenerational inequalities. The cultural imperative to own a home remains strong, yet the pathway to achieving it has become increasingly fraught with financial risk and uncertainty. In this sense, debt as destiny is not merely an individual challenge but a structural issue embedded in the design of contemporary housing markets.

Alternative models of real estate investment offer contrasting approaches that prioritise liquidity and income generation over debt accumulation. Real Estate Investment Trusts (REITs), for example, allow investors to participate in property markets without the encumbrances of mortgages or maintenance. By focusing on cash flow rather than capital appreciation tied to leverage, these vehicles provide a more flexible and accessible means of building wealth. Recognising the limitations of debt-driven homeownership opens the door to such innovations and invites a reevaluation of what it means to invest in real estate strategically.

This reexamination also has ethical and social dimensions. The mortgage-industrial complex's emphasis on debt raises questions about the equity and sustainability of housing as a fundamental human need. When access to shelter depends on the willingness and ability to assume significant debt, the resulting system can exclude vulnerable populations and perpetuate economic disparities. It prompts a broader discussion about the role of policy in balancing homeownership promotion with protections against over-indebtedness and financial precarity.

Ultimately, the concept of debt as destiny reframes the homeownership ideal by revealing the heavy costs embedded within its conventional model. It challenges the notion that buying a house is invariably a step toward financial liberation, highlighting instead how it often entails long-term obligations that restrict freedom. Understanding this dynamic equips readers to approach real estate investment with greater critical awareness and to consider alternative strategies that align better with goals of liquidity, control, and sustainable wealth accumulation. This perspective is essential for navigating the complexities of modern real estate markets and for constructing portfolios that reflect both personal aspirations and economic realities.

The Cost of Control

Owning real estate is often equated with having control—over one's environment, finances, and future. The sense of autonomy that comes with holding the deed to a property is deeply ingrained in cultural and economic narratives. Yet, this perceived control is frequently illusory. Beneath the surface of ownership lies a complex web of risks, responsibilities, and vulnerabilities that can swiftly undermine the very stability and power it promises. This subchapter exposes how the conventional understanding of control in real estate is fraught with hidden costs and how ownership can, paradoxically, become a form of entrapment rather than empowerment.

The most glaring challenge to the illusion of control manifests in market volatility. Real estate is often regarded as a stable, appreciating asset class, but history paints a more nuanced picture. The Global Financial Crisis of 2008 offers a case study in how ownership can unravel overnight. Properties that had symbolised security became liabilities as housing prices plummeted by 30% or more in many markets, leaving homeowners with negative equity and triggering a cascade of foreclosures. The very asset meant to secure one's financial future turned into a source of profound vulnerability. This episode underscored a fundamental truth: control over physical property does not shield owners from systemic economic forces. Market crashes do not discriminate between landlord and renter; ownership does not guarantee immunity from loss.

Beyond macroeconomic shocks, the day-to-day realities of property ownership reveal further complexities. Legal liabilities are an often overlooked but significant aspect of control's cost. Property owners are subject to a variety of regulations, zoning laws, and safety requirements, and failure to comply can result in costly fines or litigation. For example, landlords must navigate tenant rights laws, health and safety codes, and eviction processes that vary widely by jurisdiction. These legal frameworks create an environment where "control" requires continuous vigilance, expertise, and often, professional assistance. The myth that owners can unilaterally dictate the terms of their property use dissolves under the weight of regulatory obligations and potential disputes.

Maintenance and unforeseen disasters compound these challenges. Properties, unlike financial instruments, are physical assets subject to wear and tear, environmental damage, and obsolescence. The unexpected replacement of a roof, a burst pipe, or the discovery of structural issues can impose thousands of pounds in expenses with little warning. Such costs are not merely financial; they disrupt daily life, drain mental energy, and often necessitate difficult decisions about cash flow and priorities. Homeowners bear full responsibility for upkeep, and unlike other asset classes, the value of their investment can deteriorate rapidly if maintenance is deferred or mishandled.

Consider, for instance, the 2017 Grenfell Tower tragedy in London. Beyond the immediate human and social costs, the incident highlighted the risks associated with property ownership and management, particularly in high-density housing. Owners and managers faced intense scrutiny, legal challenges, and financial liabilities tied to regulatory compliance failures. This example illustrates that control is not merely about possession but about navigating complex responsibilities and potential liabilities that can have severe financial and reputational consequences.

The narrative of control also obscures the illiquidity inherent in physical property ownership. Unlike stocks or bonds, real estate transactions are often lengthy and costly, limiting an owner's ability to respond swiftly to changing personal or market conditions. This rigidity can trap investors in unfavourable circumstances, forcing them to hold depreciating assets or accept losses during forced sales. The transaction costs—legal fees, taxes, agent commissions—are substantial and often unpredictable. This lack of flexibility is a critical but frequently unacknowledged cost of control.

Moreover, the emotional and psychological dimensions of ownership contribute to its complexity. Property is deeply personal, often tied to identity and family history, making financial decisions more fraught. The attachment to a physical home can cause owners to resist necessary actions such as selling or diversifying their holdings, even when such decisions would be rational from an investment perspective. This cognitive bias, sometimes referred to as the "home bias," limits portfolio optimisation and exposes owners to concentrated risk.

Contrasting ownership with alternative investment vehicles clarifies these costs. Real Estate Investment Trusts (REITs), for example, offer exposure to property markets without the burdens of direct management, legal liabilities, or illiquidity. Investors gain access to diversified portfolios of income-producing real estate with the convenience of tradable securities. This model challenges traditional notions of control by prioritising economic participation over physical possession, demonstrating that control over outcomes need not require control over assets in the conventional sense.

Nonetheless, it is important to acknowledge that some degree of control can be valuable and desirable, especially for those who appreciate the tangible and experiential aspects of owning property. Yet, recognising the true costs and limits of this control is essential for informed decision-making. Ownership is not a guarantee of stability or freedom; it is a commitment that demands ongoing management, exposes one to significant risks, and can restrict financial agility.

Understanding the cost of control reframes the concept of real estate ownership from an unqualified good to a nuanced trade-off. It invites investors to weigh the emotional and symbolic value of physical possession against the practical demands and vulnerabilities it entails. This perspective encourages a more strategic approach to building wealth in real estate—one that considers not just the allure of ownership but the full spectrum of responsibilities and risks involved. By doing so, readers are better prepared to evaluate their investment choices critically and to seek models of participation that align with their goals, resources, and tolerance for complexity.

Reframing Real Estate as Cash Flow

The traditional image of real estate investment is inseparable from notions of location, lifestyle, and tangible property. For decades, prospective investors have been encouraged to think in terms of square footage, curb appeal, and neighbourhood desirability. These metrics, while intuitively understandable, often overshadow the financial fundamentals that truly define successful real estate investing. This subchapter advances a fundamental shift in perspective: real estate must be understood not as a physical asset tied to geography or aesthetics, but as a yield-producing financial vehicle—an income-generating asset class. Embracing this reframing is essential for modern investors seeking to optimise returns, manage risk, and unlock the full potential of real estate in their portfolios.

The allure of location and lifestyle is understandable; physical property is a sensory, experiential asset. Yet, the fixation on these qualities frequently leads to misplaced emphasis on capital appreciation over income generation. Real estate's intrinsic value lies not in the bricks and mortar themselves but in their capacity to produce cash flow—rental income, lease payments, and dividends—that ultimately sustains and grows wealth. This insight shifts the investor's focus from square footage to yield, from possession to participation in recurring revenue streams. Such a transition from asset as possession to asset as income stream is not merely semantic; it realigns investment strategies with the economic realities that drive value.

Consider the distinction between a luxury home in a high-demand area and a modestly sized commercial property with long-term tenants and stable cash flow. While the former may command attention for its location and potential appreciation, the latter often offers more predictable and immediate financial benefits. Investors fixated on aesthetics or personal use may overlook the superior performance characteristics of income-focused assets, which can provide steady returns regardless of market volatility. This perspective encourages a disciplined, data-driven approach to real estate, prioritising metrics such as net operating income, capitalization rates, and dividend yields over subjective qualities.

The evolution of real estate markets and financial instruments reinforces the importance of this reframing. The rise of Real Estate Investment Trusts (REITs) exemplifies the shift toward cash flow orientation. REITs pool capital to invest in diversified property portfolios that generate consistent rental income, distributing profits to shareholders as dividends. This structure abstracts the investor from physical property ownership, replacing it with participation in a liquid, transparent income stream. REITs demonstrate that real estate investment need not be tethered to physical maintenance, tenant management, or illiquidity, enabling broader access to real estate's cash flow potential.

Moreover, analysing real estate through the lens of cash flow invites a more nuanced understanding of risk. Traditional focus on property appreciation often overlooks the cyclical and regional volatility inherent in real estate markets. Income-generating assets provide a stabilising influence, as rental revenues can offset price fluctuations and provide a buffer during downturns. For instance, during periods of economic contraction, tenants with long-term leases continue to pay rent, supporting asset valuations and investor returns. This defensive characteristic of income-focused real estate can enhance portfolio resilience, especially when contrasted with speculative appreciation bets.

The conceptual shift to cash flow also aligns with broader principles of sound investment management. Modern portfolio theory emphasises diversification, liquidity, and income generation as cornerstones of risk-adjusted returns. Real estate, when approached as a cash flow asset, integrates seamlessly into diversified portfolios, complementing equities and fixed income. It provides both income and potential capital appreciation, but crucially, income that can be reinvested or deployed according to an investor's evolving needs.

This dynamic positions real estate not as a static, illiquid holding but as a versatile component of strategic asset allocation.

Critically, reframing real estate in terms of income challenges entrenched behavioural biases. The 'home bias'—the tendency for investors to overweight domestic real estate or their own homes in portfolios—is often driven by emotional attachment rather than rational assessment of cash flow potential or risk. By emphasising yield and economic fundamentals, investors can transcend such biases, adopting a more objective, evidence-based approach. This mindset is particularly important in an age where global real estate markets and financial products offer unprecedented access and diversification opportunities beyond traditional boundaries.

The practical implications of this reframing extend to how investors evaluate and select real estate opportunities. Instead of prioritising aesthetics or speculative price movements, successful investors scrutinise metrics such as occupancy rates, lease durations, tenant creditworthiness, operating expenses, and capital expenditure requirements. They understand that a well-located but poorly managed property with unstable cash flow can be a financial liability, while a less glamorous asset with reliable income streams can generate superior long-term wealth. This shift requires a deeper engagement with financial analysis and market dynamics, moving beyond surface-level appeal.

Furthermore, this cash flow-centric perspective invites a reconsideration of what ownership means. Ownership no longer necessitates hands-on management or direct control over physical assets. Instead, it can mean holding a stake in income-producing vehicles—REITs, property funds, or syndications—that delegate operational responsibilities to professional managers. This delegation reduces the burdens of property management and maintenance, freeing investors to focus on portfolio strategy and capital allocation. It transforms real estate from a burdensome possession into a scalable, efficient investment channel.

Ethically and socially, viewing real estate as cash flow also invites reflection on the role of property investment in community and economic development. Income-producing real estate supports infrastructure, provides housing, and sustains businesses. When investors prioritise stable, responsible income generation, they are inherently incentivised to maintain and improve properties, ensuring long-term viability and benefit to tenants and communities. This alignment contrasts with speculative models that may promote neglect or rapid turnover, highlighting how the cash flow framework fosters sustainable investment practices.

Reframing real estate as a cash flow asset class ultimately reshapes the investor's relationship with property. It calls for a disciplined, analytical mindset that values income, diversification, and liquidity. It challenges emotional attachments to physical space and advocates for a strategic, opportunity-focused approach. By adopting this perspective, investors can unlock the true power of real estate—consistent income that supports financial independence and portfolio growth without the encumbrances traditionally associated with ownership. This foundational shift is at the heart of contemporary real estate investing and essential for anyone seeking to build resilient, income-focused portfolios in today's complex markets.

Chapter 2
What REITs Really Are—and Why They Exist

The landscape of real estate ownership has quietly but profoundly shifted, moving from an arena reserved for the wealthy to one accessible to a far broader spectrum of investors. For centuries, wealth creation in property demanded substantial upfront capital: buying land or buildings outright was the only path, tying financial growth directly to possession. Yet beneath this longstanding model, a subtle revolution has taken root, reshaping access to real estate markets. At the heart of this transformation lie Real Estate Investment Trusts, or REITs—financial structures that package property assets into tradable securities, offering participation without the burdens of direct ownership. To fully grasp their significance, one must consider the political, economic, and legal forces that enabled their creation, the sophisticated frameworks through which they operate, and the way they usher real estate into a modern, digitised era.

REITs trace their origins to legislative innovation designed to widen investment access and stimulate economic growth. In the United States, the Real Estate Investment Trust Act of 1960 emerged from recognition that high capital requirements and illiquidity had long barred average investors from property markets. The act introduced REITs as vehicles that combined property ownership's benefits with the liquidity and transparency of publicly traded securities. By requiring these entities to distribute a significant portion of taxable income to shareholders, lawmakers ensured a reliable income stream while avoiding double taxation—aligning incentives across the capital structure. Beyond finance, this legislation was a social milestone, expanding access to real estate wealth that had traditionally been the preserve of elites.

Investing in a REIT requires a shift in understanding what is actually owned. Unlike direct property ownership, shares in a REIT represent fractional interests in a professionally managed portfolio of real estate assets. Investors participate in rental income and capital appreciation without the operational responsibilities of landlords. The structure involves pooling capital to acquire and manage income-generating properties—from office blocks and shopping centres to healthcare facilities and data centres. Adherence to regulatory criteria, including asset composition, income sources, and mandatory distributions, ensures tax advantages and enforces transparency. For the investor, this structure blends income, diversification, and professional management, while insulating them from the operational risks inherent in direct ownership.

The rise of REITs also exemplifies a broader trend: the virtualisation of property ownership. What was once a purely tangible, illiquid asset is now accessible through digital trading platforms. REIT shares can be bought or sold with relative ease, granting investors flexibility to adjust exposure in response to market conditions. Liquidity—often scarce in conventional property markets—becomes the new form of leverage, allowing capital access and risk management in ways traditional ownership cannot. This challenges conventional notions of possession, replacing them with participation and rights conveyed through a digital medium.

Trust and transparency underpin the REIT model. Regulatory oversight imposes strict reporting standards, including comprehensive financial disclosures, governance protocols, and risk management requirements. These obligations foster investor confidence, addressing barriers that historically limited broad market participation. Furthermore, the legal requirement to distribute most income as dividends ensures predictable returns, appealing to income-focused investors. By aligning management incentives with shareholder interests, REITs cultivate sustainable performance and prudent risk-taking.

Practical experience demonstrates REITs' resilience and strategic value. During periods of economic turbulence—whether the global financial crisis or recent market shocks—REITs have often provided stable income streams and maintained liquidity where direct property investments faltered. Diversified asset bases, professional oversight, and regulatory safeguards allow these vehicles to navigate volatility more adeptly than many individual property owners. Such performance enhances their appeal as a core element of diversified investment portfolios.

Yet REITs are not without limitations. Market pricing can fluctuate independently of underlying property values, influenced by broader equity market sentiment or interest rate movements. While they democratise access, they often focus on commercial and institutional-grade properties, potentially limiting exposure to residential or alternative asset classes. Informed due diligence is therefore essential: understanding both the strengths and contextual constraints of REIT investments is critical for strategic decision-making.

This chapter provides a detailed exploration of REITs—their origins, architecture, and contemporary role. By tracing the legislative, economic, and operational innovations that made them possible, readers gain clarity on what they truly own when investing in these instruments. REITs are more than financial products; they are pivotal actors in the ongoing evolution of real estate investment, bridging the divide between tangible assets and modern capital markets, and expanding access to property wealth in ways that were once unimaginable.

A Quiet Revolution in Property Ownership

The emergence of Real Estate Investment Trusts (REITs) represents one of the most significant yet underappreciated shifts in the architecture of property ownership. Unlike the well-known narratives of property markets defined by tangible bricks-and-mortar acquisitions, REITs have quietly revolutionised access to real estate, dismantling traditional barriers that long confined wealth generation to those with substantial capital. This transformation is neither accidental nor purely financial; it is the product of deliberate political, economic, and legal forces converging to democratise real estate investment and align it with the broader evolution of capital markets. Understanding this quiet revolution requires an examination of the conditions that precipitated the birth of REITs, the systemic challenges they addressed, and their ongoing impact on how property is owned and perceived.

In the mid-20th century, the real estate market was largely the preserve of wealthy individuals, institutional investors, or corporations capable of deploying large sums to acquire physical property outright. For the average investor, participation was limited by prohibitive costs, illiquidity, and the complex management responsibilities associated with direct ownership. Real estate was viewed as an asset class that promised long-term appreciation and income but was fundamentally inaccessible due to its size, indivisibility, and operational demands. This exclusivity not only restricted wealth creation but also constrained the flow of capital necessary for broader economic development, particularly in commercial and industrial real estate sectors.

The post-war economic environment set the stage for change. Growing demand for commercial infrastructure and housing combined with expanding capital markets exposed inefficiencies and highlighted the need for more inclusive investment mechanisms. Against this backdrop, policymakers and financial innovators sought solutions that could bridge the gap between real estate's potential as an income-generating asset and the desire to open markets to a wider base of investors. The response was the creation of a legal framework that would allow collective investment in real estate with the liquidity and transparency characteristics of publicly traded securities.

The United States' Real Estate Investment Trust Act of 1960 stands as a landmark in this regard. By adapting the principles underlying mutual funds and investment trusts to the real estate sector, lawmakers introduced REITs as vehicles that would pool investor capital to acquire and manage diversified property portfolios. A crucial innovation was the requirement that REITs distribute at least 90% of taxable income to shareholders, which preserved the pass-through taxation status and avoided the double taxation typically associated with corporations. This legislative design aligned investor interests around income generation while promoting transparency and regulatory oversight—a balance that encouraged broad market participation without sacrificing fiduciary responsibility.

Beyond the legislative mechanics, the political motivations behind REITs reflect broader social and economic ambitions. The democratisation of real estate investing was framed as a way to enhance economic equity, provide individual investors with access to stable income streams, and stimulate capital formation in critical sectors such as housing, retail, and infrastructure. This ethos positioned REITs not merely as financial instruments but as tools of inclusive growth, expanding the benefits of real estate ownership beyond traditional elites. The timing was also critical; the rise of institutional investing and the growth of pension funds demanded new asset classes that could deliver reliable returns and diversification, further embedding REITs within the fabric of modern capital markets.

Economically, REITs addressed several persistent challenges inherent in direct real estate investment. Illiquidity, concentrated risk, and high entry costs often deterred individuals from engaging in property markets. REITs mitigated these by offering fractional ownership, professional management, and tradability on stock exchanges. This innovation lowered barriers to entry, enhanced portfolio diversification, and introduced price discovery mechanisms absent in private property transactions. Investors could now tailor exposure to real estate with the same ease and sophistication applied to equities and bonds, fundamentally altering investment paradigms.

The expansion of REITs beyond the United States reflects their adaptability and relevance. Countries across Europe, Asia, and emerging markets have developed their own regulatory frameworks inspired by the US model, customised to local legal and economic contexts. This global diffusion underscores the universal challenges of real estate investing and the shared demand for instruments that reconcile property's inherent characteristics with modern financial expectations. In doing so, REITs have become a vital channel for capital flows, infrastructure development, and wealth creation worldwide.

Yet, the revolution is not without its complexities and critiques. Some argue that the public market orientation of REITs subjects real estate to stock market volatility, sometimes disconnecting valuations from underlying asset performance. Others highlight the tendency of REIT portfolios to concentrate in commercial real estate, potentially limiting exposure to residential or alternative sectors with different risk-return profiles. Additionally, the reliance on income distributions can create pressures on management decisions, occasionally leading to trade-offs between short-term payouts and long-term capital growth.

These tensions, however, do not diminish the profound shift REITs represent. They embody a fundamental redefinition of property ownership—from exclusive, physical possession to inclusive, financial participation. This transition reflects broader societal trends towards digitisation, liquidity, and portfolio diversification, aligning real estate with the dynamics of contemporary capital markets. Investors are no longer confined to single properties or local markets but can access a diversified range of real estate assets globally, with the added benefits of professional management and regulatory oversight.

This chapter explores the origins and evolution of this quiet revolution in property ownership. It examines the political and economic forces that shaped the REIT framework, the legal innovations that underpinned its structure, and the ways in which it has reshaped access to real estate wealth. By tracing this narrative, readers gain a nuanced understanding of how REITs emerged as pivotal instruments for modern investors—balancing inclusivity, income generation, and transparency—and why they continue to redefine what it means to own real estate in today's financial landscape.

The Structure Behind the Structure

Investing in a Real Estate Investment Trust (REIT) often conjures the image of owning physical property without the associated hassles of maintenance or tenancy disputes. Yet, the reality of what one "owns" when purchasing REIT shares is far more nuanced and anchored in a complex organisational and legal architecture. To appreciate the true nature of REIT investment, it is essential to unpack the anatomy of a REIT—how it operates, how it is taxed, and how it generates and distributes income. This understanding clarifies the economic realities behind the seemingly straightforward concept of property investment through publicly traded vehicles, providing investors with the insight needed to navigate this asset class with confidence.

At its core, a REIT is a company that owns, operates, or finances income-producing real estate. Unlike direct property ownership, where individuals hold deeds to physical assets, REIT investors hold shares in a corporation or trust that collectively owns and manages a diversified portfolio of properties. These portfolios typically span commercial office buildings, shopping centres, residential complexes, industrial warehouses, healthcare facilities, and increasingly, specialised sectors like data centres or infrastructure assets. This pooled ownership model spreads risk and grants investors access to professional management teams responsible for property acquisition, maintenance, leasing, and disposition decisions. Understanding this collective dynamic is crucial: when investing in a REIT, one is buying an interest in a business enterprise that manages real estate assets, not direct property itself.

The operational framework of REITs is governed by a series of legal and regulatory requirements designed to align the interests of investors, companies, and tax authorities. A defining characteristic of REITs is their special tax status. Provided they comply with certain criteria, REITs avoid corporate income tax by distributing at least 90% of their taxable income to shareholders annually in the form of dividends. This pass-through treatment is pivotal, as it prevents the double taxation that plagues conventional corporations—where earnings are taxed at the corporate level and again upon distribution to shareholders. This structure effectively positions REIT dividends as a primary mechanism for returning income to investors, making yield a central consideration in evaluating these investments.

However, the requirement to distribute such a high percentage of income introduces operational complexities. Since REITs retain limited earnings for reinvestment, they often rely on external financing or equity issuance to fund acquisitions or capital improvements. This dynamic creates a balancing act between maintaining steady dividend payouts and pursuing growth strategies, affecting how management allocates capital and manages leverage. Investors must recognise that while REITs deliver income consistently, their ability to compound returns through retained earnings is constrained compared to traditional companies. This tension influences valuation, risk profiles, and long-term performance trajectories.

Examining the nature of ownership further reveals a conceptual shift from tangible assets to financial interests. Shareholders in a REIT do not possess deeds or direct control over individual properties; instead, they hold equity in the REIT entity, entitling them to a share of the trust's or company's earnings and potential capital appreciation. This distinction is vital for understanding both rights and limitations. Unlike direct property owners, REIT investors cannot dictate property management decisions, nor do they bear direct responsibility for liabilities such as maintenance costs or tenant disputes. Conversely, they benefit from diversification across multiple assets and geographical locations, reducing concentration risk inherent in single-property investments.

The corporate governance of REITs further reflects this structure. Boards of directors or trustees oversee management teams, enforcing fiduciary duties to act in shareholders' best interests. Regulatory bodies impose disclosure and compliance standards that enhance transparency, ensuring investors have access to comprehensive financial and operational information. This framework contributes to trust and confidence, crucial elements given that REIT ownership is mediated through securities rather than physical assets. Investors must appreciate that this model places emphasis on governance quality, management expertise, and regulatory adherence as drivers of performance and risk mitigation.

A practical understanding of how REITs pay dividends is indispensable. Dividends are typically sourced from rental income generated by leased properties, net of operating expenses, financing costs, and capital expenditures. This income is passed on to shareholders regularly—often quarterly—making REITs attractive for income-oriented investors seeking steady cash flow. However, not all dividends are created equal. Some portion may represent return of capital rather than earnings, impacting tax treatment and investor returns. Comprehensive analysis of dividend composition and sustainability is therefore essential when evaluating REIT investments.

Taxation on the investor side introduces additional complexity. While REITs avoid corporate tax, dividends distributed to investors are generally taxed as ordinary income rather than at preferential capital gains rates. This treatment can affect after-tax returns depending on the investor's tax bracket and jurisdiction. Certain accounts, such as tax-advantaged retirement plans, may mitigate this burden. Furthermore, international investors face additional considerations including withholding taxes and treaty provisions. A sophisticated approach to taxation enhances the strategic deployment of REIT investments within broader portfolios.

Beyond the tax and income mechanics, the structure of REITs facilitates liquidity and market accessibility. Shares of publicly listed REITs trade on stock exchanges, enabling investors to buy and sell with relative ease compared to direct real estate transactions. This liquidity provides flexibility to adjust exposure, realise gains, or reallocate capital without the lengthy processes associated with property sales. It also introduces market pricing dynamics, subjecting REIT shares to equity market sentiment and macroeconomic factors, which can create volatility independent of underlying asset performance. Awareness of these market behaviours is critical for informed investment decisions.

The anatomy of REITs also reveals sectoral specialisations that influence operational and financial characteristics. Equity REITs focus on owning and managing properties, generating income through rent. Mortgage REITs, by contrast, invest in real estate debt, earning returns from interest payments. Hybrid REITs combine both approaches. Each type carries distinct risk and return profiles, capital structures, and sensitivity to interest rates and economic cycles. Investors benefit from understanding these variations to tailor allocations aligned with their investment objectives and risk tolerance.

Finally, the structural design of REITs underscores a broader evolution in real estate investing—from direct, hands-on property management to financialised ownership accessible to a wide range of investors. This shift parallels trends in other asset classes where digitisation, pooling of capital, and regulatory innovation have lowered entry barriers and enhanced portfolio construction capabilities. Recognising that REIT shares represent ownership in a managed, regulated, and income-distributing entity rather than direct possession of property reorients investor expectations and strategies.

In sum, the structure behind a REIT is a sophisticated blend of corporate governance, tax policy, financial engineering, and regulatory oversight, all calibrated to deliver income, liquidity, and diversification. For the investor, understanding these layers is crucial to appreciating what they truly own, how returns are generated and taxed, and the dynamics that govern performance. This clarity enables more informed decisions, better risk management, and a deeper appreciation of REITs as distinct yet powerful instruments in the landscape of real estate investment.

From Concrete to Code: Real Estate in the Digital Age

Real estate has long been defined by its physicality—a tangible asset rooted in land, buildings, and location. Ownership was traditionally measured in deeds, mortgages, and occupancy rights, deeply tied to concrete structures and geographic boundaries. Yet, the digital revolution has quietly but decisively reshaped this paradigm, ushering in a new era where real estate ownership transcends bricks and mortar to exist increasingly as code, data, and tradable securities. Central to this transformation are Real Estate Investment Trusts (REITs), which embody the virtualization of property ownership, converting illiquid, indivisible physical assets into liquid, fractionalised investments accessible to a broad spectrum of investors. This subchapter explores how REITs exemplify this profound shift, examining the implications of liquidity as the new leverage and the evolving nature of real estate investment in the digital age.

The traditional real estate investor was once confined by the realities of physical possession—properties were bulky, expensive, and slow to transact. Selling a building involved protracted negotiations, legal complexities, and significant transaction costs. The illiquidity of physical property constrained investor agility, often locking capital into static, single-asset exposures that were difficult to diversify or adjust quickly in response to changing market conditions. This lack of fluidity magnified risks and limited participation to those with considerable capital and operational expertise. The entry barriers inherent in direct real estate ownership contributed to a concentration of property wealth and inhibited broad-based inclusion.

REITs fundamentally alter this dynamic by converting ownership from a physical, indivisible asset into a digital security. Shares in REITs represent fractional interests in a diversified portfolio of income-producing properties, traded on public stock exchanges with relative ease. This shift to tradable securities enables investors to access real estate markets with unprecedented liquidity and flexibility. Instead of committing substantial capital to a single property and waiting months or years to divest, investors can buy or sell REIT shares in moments, responding swiftly to market signals or personal financial needs. This liquidity effectively becomes a new form of leverage, amplifying the capacity to deploy capital efficiently and manage risk dynamically.

This virtualization mirrors transformations seen across other asset classes, where digitisation has lowered barriers, increased transparency, and enabled fractional ownership. Just as equities replaced private ownership of companies, and cryptocurrencies introduced new paradigms of digital assets, REITs translate real estate into a digital format that is more accessible and responsive. The implications extend beyond convenience; liquidity reduces transaction costs, broadens investor participation, and fosters more efficient price discovery. Market valuations of REIT shares continuously incorporate available information, reflecting changing fundamentals faster than traditional property appraisals or sales.

Yet, this evolution also raises important conceptual tensions. While liquidity provides flexibility, it introduces exposure to market sentiment and volatility that are distinct from the underlying physical assets. REIT share prices can fluctuate with equity market cycles, interest rate changes, or macroeconomic developments, sometimes diverging from the intrinsic value of the properties themselves. Investors must therefore balance the benefits of liquidity with an understanding of market dynamics and potential dislocations. This contrasts with direct ownership, where property values move more slowly but are less influenced by short-term market noise.

Beyond liquidity, the digitalisation of real estate ownership enables innovative financial instruments and portfolio strategies. Investors can access sector-specific REITs focused on data centres, healthcare facilities, or logistics hubs—assets that were once difficult to acquire individually. Geographic diversification across regions and countries is similarly facilitated, overcoming the localisation constraints of direct property ownership. Moreover, technology platforms and data analytics empower more sophisticated risk assessment and asset management, further professionalising the investment process. This integration of digital tools enhances both transparency and operational efficiency.

The shift from concrete to code also reflects broader societal and economic trends. As capital markets evolve, investors increasingly seek assets that deliver predictable income streams alongside growth potential, within structures that allow for rapid reallocation and risk control. REITs, by packaging real estate into liquid securities, meet these demands effectively. They align with the preferences of modern investors—whether institutional pension funds, retail investors, or wealth managers—who prioritise scalability, diversification, and access to global markets. This alignment underpins the rapid growth and acceptance of REITs worldwide.

However, digitisation and liquidity are not panaceas. The abstraction of ownership into shares and codes may distance investors from the tangible realities of property, potentially obscuring operational risks such as tenant default, property maintenance, or regulatory changes. It requires investors to rely heavily on professional management and governance structures. The challenge lies in balancing the benefits of virtual ownership with informed due diligence and active engagement to ensure underlying asset quality and strategy alignment.

Furthermore, the digital age raises questions about the future trajectory of real estate ownership beyond REITs. Emerging technologies such as blockchain and tokenisation promise to further fractionalise and democratise property investment, enabling peer-to-peer transactions and enhanced transparency. These innovations may accelerate the move from traditional deeds to digital tokens, increasing liquidity and opening real estate markets to even broader participation. While these developments remain nascent, they underscore the ongoing transformation of property ownership from physical possession to digital participation.

In sum, the story of REITs is a story of real estate's evolution from concrete to code—a transition that recasts ownership as a fluid, tradable economic interest rather than a fixed, physical asset. Liquidity emerges as the new leverage, empowering investors with agility and access once unimaginable in property markets. This shift demands a recalibration of investment thinking, recognising the interplay between tangible asset fundamentals and digital market dynamics. Embracing this paradigm equips investors to harness the opportunities of the digital age while navigating its complexities with clarity and confidence.

Trust, Transparency, and Yield

At the heart of Real Estate Investment Trusts (REITs) lies a carefully engineered balance: delivering consistent income to investors while operating within a framework of rigorous oversight and accountability. This balance is not incidental but foundational, embedding trust and transparency directly into the structure of REITs. Unlike many private real estate investments, where opacity and illiquidity often leave investors vulnerable, REITs function within highly regulated environments that prioritise disclosure, governance, and income distribution. Understanding how these elements intertwine is essential for appreciating why REITs have become a trusted vehicle for real estate investment—and how they manage the complex dynamics between risk and yield.

The regulatory architecture governing REITs is designed to protect investors by imposing strict operational, reporting, and financial requirements. Originating with the U.S. Real Estate Investment Trust Act of 1960, these regulations have evolved to ensure that REITs maintain their intended role as income-generating investment vehicles rather than speculative enterprises. Central to this regulation is the requirement that REITs distribute at least 90% of their taxable income to shareholders annually. This mandate anchors REITs firmly in the realm of yield-focused investments, compelling them to channel most earnings directly to investors rather than accumulating profits internally. This payout obligation fosters a dependable income stream, a defining feature that distinguishes REITs from other real estate or equity investments.

The mandatory distribution rule, however, also introduces operational discipline. Since REITs must pay out the bulk of their taxable income, they typically retain minimal earnings for reinvestment, necessitating access to external capital markets to fund acquisitions or development projects. This dynamic imposes a governance framework where management's capital allocation decisions are subject to shareholder scrutiny and market discipline. Investors rely on transparent financial reporting and regular disclosures to assess whether management balances dividend stability with growth prospects responsibly. The transparency mandated by securities regulators—through quarterly financial statements, annual reports, and mandatory disclosures—ensures investors remain informed of REITs' performance, risks, and strategies, reinforcing trust in their stewardship.

Transparency extends beyond financial reporting. Regulatory frameworks often require detailed disclosures concerning property valuations, lease expirations, tenant concentrations, and debt levels. These data points are crucial for evaluating risk exposure and yield sustainability. For instance, a REIT heavily concentrated in a single tenant or property type presents different risk characteristics than a diversified portfolio spread across multiple sectors and geographies. Investors use this information to perform due diligence and construct portfolios aligned with their risk tolerance and income objectives. The granular insight provided by transparency enables a market mechanism where price discovery reflects real asset performance and risk factors, mitigating information asymmetry that historically disadvantaged real estate investors.

Trust in REITs is also rooted in their legal and governance structures. Many REITs are organised as publicly traded corporations or trusts, subject to the oversight of independent boards tasked with safeguarding shareholder interests. Fiduciary responsibilities compel boards and management to adhere to prudent financial practices, risk management protocols, and ethical standards. Regulatory bodies such as the Securities and Exchange Commission (SEC) in the United States enforce compliance through audits, reporting requirements, and enforcement actions. This multilayered oversight distinguishes REITs from less regulated private real estate vehicles, providing a degree of investor protection and confidence critical for attracting capital.

Risk management within REITs encompasses both operational and financial dimensions. Operationally, professional management teams oversee property maintenance, tenant relations, and leasing strategies to maximise income stability and asset value. Financially, REITs employ leverage cautiously, balancing debt levels to optimise returns while maintaining access to credit markets. Disclosure of leverage ratios and debt maturities is standard practice, enabling investors to assess solvency risks. Additionally, many REITs maintain diversified portfolios that spread exposure across property types and regions, reducing concentration risks and smoothing income volatility. This comprehensive risk management approach is integral to sustaining the reliable yields that underpin REIT appeal.

The yield generated by REITs is a focal point for investors, often compared favourably against bonds, equities, or direct property investment. The predictability of REIT dividends, derived from contractual lease income and professional management, offers a stable cash flow component attractive to income-oriented portfolios. However, yield analysis must account for payout ratios, dividend sustainability, and growth prospects. A high dividend yield is not inherently positive if it arises from excessive distribution of capital or unsustainable income streams. Conversely, moderate yields accompanied by robust cash flow growth and prudent financial management may signal healthier investment opportunities. Transparency in earnings quality and distribution policy equips investors to differentiate between superficial yield and genuine income generation.

Real-world events underscore the importance of trust and transparency in REIT performance. During economic downturns or market stress, such as the global financial crisis or the COVID-19 pandemic, REITs with transparent operations and conservative financial practices weathered volatility more effectively, maintaining dividend payments and investor confidence. Conversely, those with opaque reporting or aggressive leverage faced scrutiny, price declines, and dividend cuts. These episodes reinforce that yield without trust and transparency is fragile, highlighting the interdependence of these factors in the REIT model.

Nonetheless, the emphasis on trust and transparency does not eliminate all risks. Market valuations of REITs remain subject to broader equity market fluctuations, interest rate movements, and sector-specific challenges. Additionally, regulatory environments evolve, potentially affecting taxation, distribution requirements, or operational constraints. Investors must remain vigilant, continuously monitoring disclosures and management communications. The robust reporting culture of REITs provides the tools for such oversight but requires investor engagement and sophistication.

In synthesising these elements, it becomes clear that REITs are not mere vehicles for passive income but structured enterprises operating within a framework that embeds trust through transparency and disciplined yield distribution. This architecture aligns incentives across stakeholders, fostering a resilient investment model that balances income generation with risk management. For investors seeking access to real estate's cash flow benefits with a high degree of oversight and accountability, understanding the regulatory and operational fabric of REITs is indispensable. It is this interplay of trust, transparency, and yield that sustains REITs' unique position in contemporary investment portfolios and defines their appeal as a modern incarnation of property ownership.

Chapter 3
REITs vs. Physical Real Estate—A Mental Model Shift

For generations, real estate investment has been synonymous with direct ownership: acquiring a tangible property, managing tenants, addressing maintenance, and weathering the full impact of market fluctuations. This traditional model possesses undeniable appeal—the sense of control it affords, the potential for capital appreciation, and the pride inherent in possession. Yet beneath its surface lie substantial burdens, both financial and operational, that can constrain flexibility and dilute returns. The advent of Real Estate Investment Trusts, or REITs, invites a fundamental shift in mindset, one that prioritises outcome-driven efficiency over asset-heavy encumbrance. This chapter examines that shift, contrasting the complexities of physical ownership with the streamlined, systematised experience of REIT investing, and drawing on real-world examples and behavioural insights to reveal why the change is more than superficial—it is transformational.

At its core, this shift can be summarised as "asset-light, outcome-heavy." Traditional investors shoulder a heavy load: securing financing, managing properties, responding to unexpected repairs, and navigating local regulatory environments. These demands often divert time and capital from core investment objectives, complicating what might otherwise be straightforward wealth-building strategies. REITs, by contrast, distil real estate investment to its economic fundamentals—yield generation and capital growth—while relieving investors of operational burdens. From busy professionals balancing multiple commitments to globally mobile individuals seeking flexible wealth exposure, REITs offer a powerful advantage: access to real estate cash flows without the distraction of management. The conversation moves from ownership stress to financial outcomes.

Beneath this practical difference lies a behavioural dimension: emotion versus system. Physical ownership often evokes strong attachments rooted in security, identity, and legacy, which can cloud judgment. Cognitive biases—loss aversion, overconfidence, the endowment effect—lead owners to retain underperforming properties, resist necessary adjustments, or act impulsively based on sentiment rather than data. REITs operate within disciplined structures, governed by transparency, automation, and performance metrics. The separation of management from ownership helps mitigate emotional interference, allowing investors to engage rationally with portfolio performance and market signals. This systemic approach promotes discipline and reduces behavioural pitfalls endemic to direct property ownership.

Leverage—borrowing to amplify returns—is another area where the mental model shift is striking. Individual property investors often assume personal debt, exposing themselves to interest rate fluctuations, liquidity crunches, and financial strain. Market downturns or cash flow interruptions can translate immediately into personal pressure. REITs, however, utilise institutional-scale leverage, accessing diverse funding sources with sophisticated risk management. Investors gain exposure to leveraged portfolios without incurring personal debt or managing credit complexities. This structure delivers the upside potential of leverage while shielding investors from many of its hazards.

Accessibility and agility further distinguish REITs from traditional ownership. Buying or selling shares can be accomplished in moments, in stark contrast to the lengthy contracts, inspections, and legal entanglements of physical property transactions. For younger investors, those in high-cost markets, or those whose lifestyles demand mobility, REITs offer a level of flexibility and liquidity that physical ownership cannot. This fluidity redefines "ownership," shifting focus from static possession to dynamic participation in income-generating assets.

Investor narratives illustrate these contrasts vividly. A mid-career professional balancing a full-time job and family commitments faces significant time and risk when managing direct properties. Allocating capital to REITs allows participation across multiple real estate sectors, quarterly income distribution, and reliance on professional managers—without disrupting daily life. Likewise, a globally mobile individual can achieve diversified income streams and portfolio stability unattainable through geographically constrained ownership. These examples underscore a mental model increasingly focused on outcomes rather than the trappings of possession.

This is not to dismiss the value or appeal of direct property ownership, which remains a valid and rewarding strategy for many. Rather, it calls for a reframing: recognising that physical ownership is but one path to real estate wealth. By emphasising liquidity, income generation, and diversification, the REIT approach challenges entrenched assumptions and expands the investor's toolkit. It underscores the truth that real estate's core value lies not in possession but in financial performance and risk management.

Throughout this chapter, these themes are explored with analytical depth and practical clarity. Behavioural dynamics influencing investment decisions are unpacked, leverage structures examined, and the role of technology and financial innovation highlighted. By the end, readers will be equipped to rethink real estate investing, embracing a mental model that privileges efficiency, discipline, and strategic flexibility—ultimately positioning them to build resilient, income-focused portfolios attuned to contemporary financial realities.

Asset-Light, Outcome-Heavy

The traditional model of real estate investing is often romanticised as a path to tangible wealth—owning a physical asset, controlling its use, and watching its value appreciate over time. Yet this model carries burdens that extend far beyond financial commitment: hands-on management, maintenance headaches, tenant relations, legal complexities, and illiquidity. These practical encumbrances impose substantial costs in time, stress, and opportunity. In stark contrast, the rise of Real Estate Investment Trusts (REITs) has ushered in a fundamentally different approach—asset-light, outcome-heavy—where the investor sheds operational responsibilities while retaining exposure to the economic benefits of real estate. This shift demands a recalibration of mental models, highlighting the trade-offs between control and convenience, complexity and clarity, and ultimately risk and reward.

Traditional real estate ownership is synonymous with the weight of responsibility. Consider the example of Sarah, a mid-career professional who purchased a residential rental property as part of her long-term wealth strategy. While the property promised steady rental income and potential appreciation, Sarah quickly found herself enmeshed in tenant disputes, emergency repairs, fluctuating local regulations, and the unpredictability of vacancy rates. Each of these factors consumed time and financial resources, often unpredictably. The illiquidity of property meant she could not easily divest when market conditions shifted, locking capital into an asset that demanded constant attention. This case illustrates a common reality: the asset is heavy not only in capital terms but in operational demands.

By contrast, REIT investing liberates individuals like Sarah from these burdens. Through purchasing shares in a REIT, investors gain access to diversified real estate portfolios professionally managed by experts. The investor's relationship with the asset is reframed: rather than managing property, they monitor performance metrics and receive dividends, outcomes generated by the underlying real estate without direct involvement in day-to-day operations. This asset-light model allows investors to focus on financial goals and portfolio strategy without being weighed down by the practicalities of ownership. The economic exposure remains intact, but the experience is streamlined and scalable.

This structural difference has profound implications for risk and reward. Physical property ownership concentrates risk in a single asset or market, amplifying vulnerability to local economic downturns, tenant defaults, or regulatory changes. The operational demands also increase exposure to unforeseen costs—maintenance emergencies, legal liabilities, or property damage—that can erode returns. REITs, by pooling assets across sectors and geographies, diffuse such risks. Professional management applies specialised expertise to tenant selection, property upkeep, and market positioning, further mitigating operational hazards. The investor's risk is primarily market and economic in nature rather than idiosyncratic or management-related, aligning with the risk profiles of other liquid securities.

An instructive comparison emerges when examining investment outcomes over time. Physical real estate may deliver episodic gains punctuated by periods of stagnation, significant cash outflows, and management challenges. REITs tend to offer more consistent income streams through mandated dividend distributions and regular portfolio rebalancing. While REIT share prices are subject to equity market volatility, their income component provides a stabilising influence. This characteristic suits investors seeking reliable cash flow and portfolio diversification, highlighting the outcome-heavy nature of REIT investing.

Critics of the asset-light model often cite the perceived loss of control as a drawback. Direct ownership confers decision-making power over property management, renovation, and tenant relations—elements many investors find appealing. Yet, this control comes at a cost: the demands of time, expertise, and emotional investment. REITs trade direct control for operational delegation, shifting authority to specialised managers and boards. This trade-off, while potentially discomfiting to some, often results in superior financial outcomes due to professional oversight, economies of scale, and disciplined governance. Moreover, regulatory frameworks and transparency requirements foster accountability, reducing agency risks inherent in delegation.

Consider the profile of James, a young digital nomad with limited capital but a desire to invest in real estate. Traditional ownership would be prohibitively complex and expensive, particularly given his mobility and lack of local knowledge. REITs offer James immediate access to real estate income and diversification with minimal effort, enabling him to align investment exposure with lifestyle flexibility. This real-world example underscores the democratizing potential of asset-light investing, opening doors previously closed to many.

This model also reflects broader societal shifts toward digitisation and convenience. Just as other asset classes have evolved through technological innovation and financial engineering, real estate investment has adapted to meet modern investor preferences. Asset-light, outcome-heavy approaches leverage data, automation, and institutional scale to optimise returns while minimising friction. The mental model shifts from hands-on stewardship to strategic capital allocation, emphasising outcomes over inputs.

In navigating the choice between physical ownership and REIT investment, it is essential to assess individual objectives, risk tolerance, and resource availability. Both approaches have merits and may coexist within diversified portfolios. Yet recognising the fundamental differences—between the burdensome weight of tangible assets and the streamlined efficiency of financial participation—enables more informed, rational decision-making. The asset-light, outcome-heavy paradigm challenges entrenched real estate myths and offers a compelling alternative aligned with the complexities of contemporary investing.

Ultimately, this shift reframes what it means to build real estate wealth. It invites investors to consider not the physical footprint of property but the financial footprint it leaves on their portfolios—cash flow, diversification, and growth potential achieved without the traditional encumbrances. Embracing this mental model equips investors to harness the power of real estate investment with agility, clarity, and efficiency, positioning them for sustainable success in an evolving market landscape.

Emotions vs. Systems

Real estate investing sits at the intersection of finance and human psychology, a nexus where rational calculation often clashes with deep-seated emotional impulses. The allure of owning physical property—its tangibility, its promise of security, its cultural symbolism—taps into powerful feelings of identity, control, and legacy. Yet, these very emotions frequently lead investors down paths fraught with cognitive biases, overconfidence, and attachment, which can undermine sound financial decision-making. In contrast, Real Estate Investment Trusts (REITs) offer a fundamentally different paradigm—one governed by disciplined systems, automation, and data-driven analysis—that mitigates emotional pitfalls and fosters consistent investment outcomes. Exploring this contrast reveals how shifting from emotions to systems is not merely prudent but essential for mastering real estate investing in the modern era.

Physical real estate investment is inherently personal. The property often becomes intertwined with an owner's self-concept and life narrative. Psychological phenomena such as the endowment effect amplify perceived value simply because one owns the asset, inflating attachment beyond market realities. This attachment can lead to reluctance in selling underperforming properties or making difficult portfolio adjustments. Anecdotal evidence abounds of homeowners holding onto real estate despite diminishing returns, resisting market signals in favour of emotional comfort. Such behaviour illustrates how emotions can distort investment logic, impeding optimal capital allocation.

Moreover, the complexity and immediacy of physical property management amplify emotional involvement. Owners confront tenant issues, maintenance emergencies, and fluctuating local policies—events that evoke stress, frustration, and urgency. These affective responses can drive impulsive decisions, such as precipitous sales during downturns or overinvestment in ill-advised renovations. Behavioural finance research confirms that such emotionally charged environments exacerbate biases like loss aversion and confirmation bias, impairing objective assessment. Unlike other asset classes, where price changes are abstract and impersonal, real estate's physical presence and operational demands intensify the emotional dimension.

REITs, by design, distance investors from this emotionally fraught terrain. Ownership in a REIT translates to shares in a professionally managed entity, where day-to-day decisions are made by experts leveraging data, market research, and established protocols. This delegation introduces systemic discipline, replacing anecdote with analytics and instinct with evidence. Automated reporting, regulatory oversight, and transparent disclosures further support rational evaluation, empowering investors to focus on measurable outcomes rather than personal sentiment. The removal of direct management responsibilities reduces cognitive load and emotional entanglement, enabling more consistent investment behaviour.

This systematisation extends to how REITs handle market volatility and operational challenges. Whereas individual owners may respond emotionally to tenant turnover or market dips with panic or inertia,

REIT management employs strategic asset allocation, risk diversification, and financial hedging to smooth performance. The presence of structured governance—boards, audits, compliance teams—introduces checks and balances that curb impulsive or shortsighted actions. Investors benefit indirectly from these institutional safeguards, which translate into steadier income streams and clearer growth trajectories.

A striking example of emotion-driven decision-making in direct ownership can be seen during real estate market cycles. Homeowners or landlords often fall prey to the 'boom-bust' mindset: exuberantly purchasing at market peaks due to fear of missing out, then delaying sales at troughs out of loss aversion or hope for recovery. This cycle amplifies financial damage and prolongs recovery periods. REIT investors, in contrast, transact within liquid markets that facilitate portfolio rebalancing and risk management. Though REIT shares are not immune to volatility, the systemic infrastructure encourages long-term discipline and reduces the temptation for reactive, emotionally charged trades.

The behavioural contrast is particularly salient when considering younger or less experienced investors. The psychological burden and complexity of direct real estate ownership can be intimidating and overwhelming, leading to suboptimal entry decisions or excessive caution. REITs, with their accessibility, transparency, and reliance on data, lower these barriers. They provide a framework where investment decisions are supported by consistent information flows, benchmark comparisons, and professional stewardship. This reduces decision fatigue and enhances confidence, encouraging participation without the emotional overhang that often accompanies physical property investment.

Critics may argue that systems lack the personal connection and control prized by many investors. While it is true that REITs abstract away direct ownership, this distance should not be conflated with disengagement. Instead, it represents a shift in how control is exercised—from hands-on management to strategic capital deployment and portfolio oversight. Investors retain agency through selection, monitoring, and allocation decisions informed by transparent data and governance. This redefinition aligns better with the realities of modern markets, where scale, complexity, and information flows demand systemic approaches.

Technological advances further reinforce this systemic paradigm. Sophisticated analytics, real-time market data, and algorithmic models empower REIT management and investors alike to base decisions on objective criteria rather than intuition. Automation in reporting and compliance ensures accuracy and timeliness, while digital platforms facilitate seamless trading and portfolio management. These innovations collectively embed rationality into the investment process, mitigating emotional biases and enhancing outcomes.

Ethically, the shift from emotions to systems also promotes fairness and inclusivity. By reducing dependence on personal networks, local knowledge, or operational capacity, REITs democratise access to real estate's economic benefits. Investors are judged less by their capacity to manage properties or negotiate deals, and more by their strategic acumen and risk tolerance. This systemic model broadens participation and fosters a more equitable investment landscape.

In examining the tension between emotions and systems, it becomes evident that emotional investment in physical property—while natural and understandable—poses significant risks to financial optimisation. REITs offer an alternative rooted in structure and discipline, enabling investors to harness real estate's potential without succumbing to behavioural pitfalls. This mental model shift from personal attachment to systemic engagement is central to navigating contemporary real estate markets effectively and building resilient, income-generating portfolios.

Ultimately, embracing systems over emotions empowers investors to transcend instinctual biases and operate with clarity and confidence. It encourages a perspective that values data integrity, transparency, and governance as cornerstones of successful investment. By doing so, investors position themselves to capture real estate's rewards in a manner consistent with sound financial principles and modern market dynamics.

Leverage, Without the Whiplash

Leverage is a double-edged sword in the world of real estate investment. While it can amplify returns and accelerate portfolio growth, it also magnifies risks, exposing investors to heightened volatility, potential losses, and financial distress. The experience of many individual property owners reveals this harsh reality: personal debt tied to real estate can become a source of whiplash, swinging investor fortunes dramatically with changing market conditions, interest rates, or income disruptions. Real Estate Investment Trusts (REITs), however, harness leverage differently—at institutional scale and with professional oversight—allowing investors to benefit from debt-enhanced returns without incurring the full brunt of personal financial risk. This nuanced deployment of leverage is a defining feature of REITs, offering what might be called "leverage without the whiplash."

Traditional real estate ownership often entails personal borrowing secured by the property itself. Mortgages, home equity loans, and other forms of debt financing enable owners to acquire assets with less upfront capital, theoretically magnifying gains if property values rise or rental income increases. Yet this model also binds the investor to fixed obligations: regular principal and interest payments, maintenance costs, and vulnerability to market downturns. Economic shocks, job losses, or interest rate hikes can rapidly transform leveraged gains into crippling losses. The 2008 financial crisis vividly illustrated this phenomenon, where widespread defaults and foreclosures arose largely due to over-leverage at the individual homeowner level. The volatility and personal liability embedded in such leverage constitute the "whiplash" that can destabilise wealth and wellbeing.

REITs operate within a fundamentally different leverage framework. As pooled investment vehicles, they access capital markets and debt financing at institutional scales, benefiting from favourable credit terms, diversified collateral, and sophisticated risk management practices. Leverage within a REIT's portfolio is managed strategically, balancing debt and equity to optimise returns while maintaining liquidity and solvency. Crucially, individual REIT investors are insulated from personal debt obligations; their exposure is limited to the market value fluctuations of REIT shares, not direct liability for underlying borrowings. This separation mitigates the risk of financial distress associated with personal leverage, delivering scaled benefits without corresponding individual vulnerabilities.

Institutional leverage within REITs is subject to rigorous governance and regulatory scrutiny. Debt levels, interest coverage ratios, and maturity profiles are regularly disclosed, enabling investors to assess leverage risk transparently. Many REITs maintain conservative leverage relative to industry norms, adhering to investment-grade credit metrics that ensure access to capital and resilience under stress. This prudent management contrasts sharply with the variable, often opaque, debt structures individual property owners face. Investors in REITs gain confidence from this transparency and oversight, reducing uncertainty and enhancing risk-adjusted returns.

The economies of scale available to REITs further differentiate their leverage profile. Large, diversified property portfolios spread debt service obligations across multiple assets, sectors, and tenants, reducing exposure to idiosyncratic shocks. Professional management teams actively monitor market conditions, refinancing strategies, and capital allocation to optimise leverage use. This dynamic management contrasts with the static, often reactive approach individual owners must adopt, who may lack expertise or flexibility to respond to changing financial environments. The REIT model thus embodies leverage as a disciplined tool, not a precarious gamble.

Leverage within REITs also interacts with their dividend distribution requirements, influencing income sustainability. Since REITs must distribute a high percentage of taxable income, reliance on debt must be carefully calibrated to support consistent cash flow without overextending financial commitments. This constraint incentivises management to avoid excessive leverage that could jeopardise dividend payments and investor confidence. Consequently, REITs often strike a balance between growth ambitions and yield preservation, aligning leverage strategies with long-term stability.

From the investor perspective, this structure offers a compelling value proposition. Individuals can access the amplified returns generated by institutional leverage without assuming personal debt or the associated volatility. This access broadens participation, allowing investors with varying capital levels and risk tolerances to benefit from real estate's leverage effects safely. For example, a retail investor buying REIT shares gains exposure to a portfolio leveraged at a scale and sophistication impossible to replicate in direct ownership without significant resources and expertise.

Nevertheless, leverage in REITs is not risk-free. Share prices remain sensitive to interest rate fluctuations, credit market conditions, and economic cycles that influence borrowing costs and asset valuations. Overleveraged REITs can experience share price declines or dividend cuts during adverse conditions. Investors must conduct due diligence, evaluating leverage ratios, debt maturities, and management's capital strategy to gauge risk appropriately. Understanding these nuances ensures leverage's benefits are harnessed without succumbing to its pitfalls.

Emerging trends in REIT financing further refine the leverage paradigm. Innovations such as green bonds, sustainable financing, and diversified credit facilities enhance capital availability and align leverage with environmental, social, and governance (ESG) criteria. These developments signal a maturing market where leverage is integrated into broader strategic objectives beyond simple return enhancement. Investors attuned to these trends can identify REITs leveraging responsibly to achieve resilient, future-oriented growth.

The contrast between personal debt-driven leverage and REIT institutional leverage crystallises a key advantage of modern real estate investing: access to sophisticated financial engineering without personal financial exposure. This distinction reflects a broader shift toward professionalised, scalable, and systematised investment models that prioritise risk management alongside return. For investors seeking real estate's growth and income potential with measured risk, understanding the architecture and implications of leverage within REITs is indispensable.

In sum, REITs offer a pathway to leverage that enhances returns without exposing individuals to the whiplash of personal debt. Through institutional scale, disciplined governance, and transparent risk management, they transform leverage from a volatile risk factor into a controlled, strategic asset. This evolution represents a critical advancement in real estate investing, reconciling ambition with prudence, and opportunity with protection—empowering investors to participate confidently in property markets underpinned by robust financial frameworks.

Owning with a Click, Not a Contract

The traditional path to real estate investment is often described in terms of contracts, legal documents, mortgages, and management responsibilities—a process that can be labyrinthine, capital-intensive, and intimidating. For many, especially younger investors, digital nomads, or those constrained by high-barrier housing markets, this traditional approach represents an almost insurmountable obstacle to participating in real estate wealth creation. Real Estate Investment Trusts (REITs) radically simplify this journey, transforming ownership into an agile, accessible experience that requires nothing more than a few clicks online. This subchapter examines how REITs dismantle barriers through technology, liquidity, and streamlined processes, opening the doors to real estate investment for a new generation and a more mobile, globalised population.

The very act of buying a property typically involves months of preparation: securing financing, legal due diligence, inspections, contract negotiations, and closing procedures. This protracted process demands not only significant capital but also time, local expertise, and administrative bandwidth. In contrast, REIT investing collapses these complexities into straightforward equity transactions conducted via stock exchanges or brokerage platforms. For a prospective investor, acquiring shares in a REIT can be as immediate as purchasing any publicly traded stock. This dramatic reduction in friction enables entry into real estate markets without geographic constraints, legal entanglements, or operational responsibilities.

Young investors, often burdened by student debt, rising living costs, and shifting career trajectories, find REITs particularly compelling. The substantial down payments and mortgage qualifications that traditional property ownership requires are frequently unattainable or financially unwise early in one's career. REITs offer a capital-efficient alternative, allowing fractional ownership with minimal initial outlay and no ongoing property management obligations. This accessibility democratizes real estate investment, providing exposure to income-generating assets and potential capital appreciation without the barriers of credit approval or physical property stewardship.

Digital nomads exemplify another demographic for whom REITs are transformative. Living fluid lives across countries and continents, these individuals often face legal and practical challenges in owning property tied to a single location. Residency requirements, local taxation, property maintenance, and rental management impose constraints incompatible with a nomadic lifestyle. REITs circumvent these issues entirely by abstracting ownership into liquid shares traded globally, enabling consistent income generation and portfolio diversification without the need to anchor oneself to physical real estate. This flexibility aligns with contemporary lifestyles characterised by mobility and digital engagement.

High-barrier housing markets—such as London, New York, or Sydney—present formidable obstacles to entry even for well-capitalised investors. Skyrocketing prices, intense competition, and regulatory hurdles can render direct ownership prohibitively expensive or strategically limiting. REITs, by pooling investor capital and operating at scale, unlock access to prime real estate markets that would otherwise be inaccessible to many. This pooled model not only lowers entry thresholds but also spreads risk across diverse properties and sectors, mitigating concentration risks endemic to individual property purchases.

The technological infrastructure supporting REIT investing enhances this ease and agility. Online brokerage platforms, mobile trading apps, and digital wallets facilitate instantaneous transactions, real-time portfolio monitoring, and streamlined dividend reinvestment. Data analytics and transparency tools empower investors to make informed decisions based on comprehensive financial and operational information. This integration of finance and technology delivers a seamless user experience, far removed from the paperwork and delays characteristic of physical property transactions.

Yet, the simplification afforded by REITs does not imply a lack of sophistication or oversight. Regulatory frameworks impose strict disclosure, governance, and reporting requirements that protect investor interests and maintain market integrity. Investors can access detailed information on asset composition, financial performance, management strategies, and risk exposures. This transparency underpins trust and allows participants—regardless of experience—to engage with real estate investment on an informed basis.

While REITs democratise access and simplify ownership, they also shift investor focus toward portfolio construction and long-term strategy. The agility to buy and sell shares quickly facilitates dynamic asset allocation and risk management, supporting goals ranging from income generation to capital growth. This contrasts with the relative inflexibility of direct property, where sales are slow and costly. The ability to adjust exposure efficiently makes REITs well suited to contemporary investment philosophies emphasizing diversification, liquidity, and responsive management.

Critics may caution that the abstraction of real estate into tradable securities distances investors from the tangible benefits and control associated with physical ownership. While direct control over properties remains the domain of some investors, many recognise that the trade-off for liquidity, diversification, and professional management aligns better with their financial and lifestyle objectives. The notion of ownership itself evolves—from possession of physical space to economic participation in income-generating assets. This conceptual shift reflects broader trends in asset ownership across industries, where digitisation and financial innovation redefine access and control.

Real-world cases illuminate these dynamics vividly. For example, millennials entering high-cost housing markets often defer or forego direct home purchases, instead allocating capital to REITs to build wealth exposure. Simultaneously, expatriates and global professionals leverage REITs to maintain diversified real estate holdings without the logistical burdens of cross-border property management. These scenarios underscore how REITs empower investors to own with a click, not a contract—embracing efficiency without sacrificing participation.

Ultimately, this evolution signals a broader democratization and modernization of real estate investment. REITs remove traditional gatekeepers and barriers, translating complex, illiquid, and capital-intensive assets into accessible, liquid securities. For investors constrained by geography, capital, or lifestyle, owning real estate through REITs is a practical, strategic choice that aligns with the demands of the 21st-century economy. Embracing this model equips investors to engage confidently with real estate's income and growth potential—without the friction, complexity, or commitments historically required by direct ownership.

Chapter 4
The Many Faces of REITs

Real estate investment has evolved far beyond the conventional confines of single-family homes, office towers, or shopping centres. Today, it presents a far more intricate and diversified universe, where Real Estate Investment Trusts (REITs) offer exposure to a multitude of property sectors—each distinguished by unique characteristics, risk profiles, and growth potential. This chapter guides the reader through the varied landscape of REIT niches—from well-established domains such as retail and industrial spaces to the rapidly expanding frontiers of data centres, healthcare facilities, and specialised sectors—revealing how these asset classes behave across economic cycles and technological shifts. Grasping this diversity is essential for investors aiming to construct portfolios that balance dependable income, capital growth, and strategic foresight.

The spectrum of REIT sectors demonstrates real estate's remarkable adaptability to shifting economic imperatives and societal trends. Retail REITs, once the backbone of commercial property, have been challenged by the rise of e-commerce and changing consumer habits, compelling operators to reinvent strategies. Industrial and logistics REITs, in contrast, have surged in relevance as global supply chains and last-mile delivery demand intensified. Healthcare REITs occupy a distinct space at the intersection of demographic pressures and regulatory complexity, encompassing properties from senior living to hospitals. Hospitality REITs, meanwhile, are acutely sensitive to economic cycles and travel trends, requiring nimble management and proactive risk mitigation. Each sector's performance is shaped by macroeconomic currents, presenting a tapestry of opportunities and pitfalls that discerning investors must interpret.

Income characteristics among REITs vary just as widely as their asset bases. Certain sectors traditionally yield high dividends, appealing to investors prioritising stable cash flows, while others channel profits back into expansion to drive future growth. The balance between dividend reliability and long-term appreciation is central to REIT strategy. For instance, retail and healthcare REITs often deliver steady income underpinned by long-term leases and essential services, whereas technology infrastructure or data centre REITs may reinvest more aggressively to capture emergent opportunities. Evaluating payout ratios, cash flow durability, and sector fundamentals is critical to aligning investor expectations with both risk tolerance and financial objectives.

Emerging specialty REITs illustrate the cutting edge of innovation in real estate investing. Green REITs focus on sustainable, energy-efficient properties, harnessing regulatory incentives and growing investor demand for environmental responsibility. Tech infrastructure REITs own assets such as cell towers, fibre networks, and data hubs, which are central to the digital economy's expansion. In jurisdictions where cannabis is legal, sector-specific REITs offer exposure to high-growth, high-risk markets with distinctive regulatory and operational challenges. These niche instruments blend traditional real estate fundamentals with sector-specific dynamics, requiring sophisticated analysis and forward-looking insight to gauge both opportunity and risk.

Some REITs operate with the dynamism and risk appetite reminiscent of startups. These entities pursue aggressive growth strategies, innovative asset classes, or emerging market opportunities, blending real estate's capital-intensive nature with entrepreneurial ventures. Such REITs may engage in development projects, strategic acquisitions, or collaborative partnerships—ventures that carry heightened uncertainty but promise disproportionate rewards. This evolution challenges the conventional perception of REITs as primarily income-oriented vehicles, demonstrating their increasingly versatile role within the broader real estate ecosystem.

This chapter examines these dimensions in depth, providing a comprehensive yet incisive perspective on the multiple faces of REITs. By illuminating sector-specific behaviours, income dynamics, and innovative niches, it equips investors to navigate complexity with discernment and construct portfolios capable of harnessing real estate's diverse potential. REITs are not a uniform instrument; they are a versatile suite of opportunities demanding thoughtful engagement, continuous learning, and strategic adaptability. Appreciating this diversity allows investors to align their portfolios with distinct objectives while responding resiliently to the shifting currents of the economic landscape.

Retail to Data Centres: A Universe of Niches

The contemporary Real Estate Investment Trust (REIT) landscape is a mosaic of specialised sectors, each reflecting distinct economic drivers, risk profiles, and growth dynamics. Far from a monolithic asset class, REITs now encompass a universe of niches—ranging from retail complexes and healthcare facilities to logistics hubs, industrial properties, hospitality venues, and cutting-edge data centres. Understanding how these sectors behave under varying economic conditions is vital for investors seeking to navigate real estate's complexity with acuity and precision. This exploration unveils the sector-specific factors shaping income stability, capital appreciation, and resilience, providing the foundation for informed portfolio construction.

Retail REITs, historically dominant in commercial real estate, exemplify the sector's evolution amid structural shifts. Traditional brick-and-mortar retail has faced significant headwinds due to the rise of e-commerce, changing consumer behaviour, and, more recently, the impacts of global health crises. Consequently, retail REITs have adapted by focusing on experiential destinations, mixed-use developments, and grocery-anchored centres that generate foot traffic resilient to online competition. The economic sensitivity of retail properties manifests in variable occupancy rates and rental concessions during downturns, making these REITs cyclical yet potentially lucrative in recovery phases. For example, in markets with robust consumer spending and tourism, retail REITs can capitalise on rebound effects, while underperforming in prolonged recessions.

Healthcare REITs occupy a uniquely defensive niche, owning assets such as hospitals, senior living facilities, medical office buildings, and specialised care centres. Driven by demographic trends—including ageing populations and increasing chronic disease prevalence—healthcare REITs tend to exhibit income stability less correlated with economic cycles. Long-term leases and government-backed reimbursements contribute to predictable cash flows, cushioning against recessions that typically dampen other real estate sectors.

However, regulatory complexities, policy shifts, and operational challenges within healthcare delivery introduce distinct risks. The nuanced balance between demographic-driven growth and regulatory exposure requires sophisticated analysis to gauge healthcare REIT performance potential.

Logistics and industrial REITs have surged to prominence amid the global expansion of e-commerce, supply chain reconfiguration, and just-in-time inventory strategies. Warehouses, distribution centres, and last-mile delivery hubs underpin modern commerce, making these assets essential infrastructure. Their performance is closely tied to trade volumes, manufacturing output, and technological innovation in logistics. While generally benefiting from secular growth trends, these REITs remain sensitive to geopolitical tensions, trade disruptions, and automation impacts. Investors must assess tenant diversification, lease durations, and geographic positioning to understand risk exposures within this sector. The dynamic growth and evolving tenant requirements differentiate logistics and industrial REITs from more static property types.

Hospitality REITs represent a highly cyclical sector, encompassing hotels, resorts, and conference centres. Their fortunes are inextricably linked to consumer discretionary spending, travel demand, and broader economic conditions. Economic expansions tend to drive occupancy rates and room pricing, while downturns prompt rapid declines. The hospitality sector also faces unique operational challenges, such as variable management quality, seasonality, and competition from alternative lodging platforms. Despite volatility, well-managed hospitality REITs can generate significant returns through active asset management, brand partnerships, and strategic location choices. Their inclusion in portfolios requires careful timing and risk appetite considerations.

Data centres constitute a relatively recent but rapidly growing REIT niche, reflecting the digital economy's infrastructure demands. These facilities house servers, network equipment, and cloud computing resources vital to internet functionality, enterprise operations, and emerging technologies like artificial intelligence. Data centre REITs benefit from robust secular trends—rising data consumption, cloud migration, and cybersecurity imperatives—that drive demand for capacity and reliability. Their income streams often feature long-term contracts with large technology firms, providing revenue visibility and growth potential. Nevertheless, these REITs confront technological obsolescence risks, high capital expenditure requirements, and energy consumption concerns. Navigating this sector requires deep understanding of technological trends and tenant creditworthiness.

These diverse sectors illustrate the heterogeneity within REITs, underscoring that real estate investing is far from a one-dimensional exercise. Each niche responds differently to economic cycles, technological disruptions, regulatory environments, and demographic shifts. For instance, while retail and hospitality REITs are more sensitive to consumer confidence and spending, healthcare and data centre REITs exhibit defensive characteristics with growth anchored in structural trends. Logistics and industrial REITs combine cyclical and secular elements, influenced by trade dynamics and innovation in supply chains.

Investors must calibrate portfolio exposure to these sectors in line with risk tolerance, income needs, and growth objectives. Diversification across sectors can mitigate volatility inherent in any single niche, while concentrated positions may exploit specialised knowledge or thematic convictions. The interplay of sector-specific factors also informs dividend sustainability and capital appreciation potential, influencing overall investment outcomes.

Moreover, sector behaviours are evolving. Retail REITs experiment with mixed-use developments to counteract e-commerce's impact; healthcare REITs adapt to telemedicine and regulatory shifts; logistics REITs invest in automation and sustainability; hospitality REITs leverage technology for customer experience; data centres pursue energy efficiency and geographic expansion. These adaptations highlight the necessity for continuous market analysis and agility in portfolio management.

In sum, the universe of REIT niches presents a rich tapestry of investment opportunities shaped by distinctive economic drivers and risk profiles. Understanding the particularities of retail, healthcare, logistics, industrial, hospitality, and data centre REITs—

and their responses to macroeconomic forces—is indispensable for constructing resilient, income-generating, and growth-oriented real estate portfolios. This sectoral insight equips investors to move beyond broad generalisations, engage deeply with asset-specific dynamics, and harness the multifaceted potential of modern real estate investing.

Income Profiles: High Yield vs. Growth

In the realm of Real Estate Investment Trusts (REITs), income is not merely a byproduct; it is a defining feature that shapes investor expectations, portfolio construction, and risk appetite. Yet, beneath the surface of steady dividend payments lies a complex spectrum of income profiles—ranging from high-yield, income-focused REITs to those prioritising growth through capital appreciation. Understanding the nuanced differences between these approaches, and how to balance dividend reliability with long-term value creation, is crucial for investors seeking to harness real estate's financial potential while managing risk effectively.

REITs are legally mandated to distribute at least 90% of their taxable income as dividends, making income generation an intrinsic part of their appeal. However, not all REITs deliver income in the same manner or with the same strategic emphasis. High-yield REITs typically operate in mature sectors—such as retail, healthcare, or certain residential properties—where stable cash flows are supported by long-term leases and essential services. These REITs attract investors prioritising predictable, steady income streams, often retirees or those seeking to supplement cash flow. The appeal lies in consistent dividend payments that can rival or exceed fixed-income instruments, coupled with potential tax advantages depending on jurisdiction and account type.

Yet, high yields come with caveats. Elevated dividend payouts may reflect slower capital growth prospects or sector-specific risks. For instance, retail REITs with high yields might face structural headwinds from e-commerce shifts, potentially pressuring future cash flows and dividend sustainability. A high yield can also signal distribution of return of capital rather than earnings, a nuance that affects long-term wealth accumulation and tax treatment. Prudent investors scrutinise payout ratios, cash flow quality, and sector fundamentals to differentiate sustainable income from superficial yield. The balance between immediate income and underlying asset health is delicate but critical.

Growth-oriented REITs, in contrast, prioritise capital appreciation by reinvesting earnings into property acquisitions, development projects, or portfolio enhancement. These REITs often belong to sectors poised for expansion or innovation, such as technology infrastructure, data centres, or certain industrial assets. Their dividend yields may be lower, reflecting the retention of earnings to fuel growth. Investors in growth REITs seek to benefit from rising asset values and expanding income streams over time, accepting lower current income in exchange for future upside. This approach aligns with longer investment horizons and a tolerance for greater volatility.

The strategic choice between high yield and growth REITs is not binary; rather, it exists along a continuum shaped by individual investor goals, risk tolerance, and market conditions. Income-focused investors might prioritise portfolio stability and cash flow, integrating high-yield REITs as core holdings. Growth-oriented investors may allocate capital toward REITs with dynamic expansion strategies, seeking capital gains alongside dividends. Blending these profiles within a diversified REIT portfolio can balance immediate income needs with capital appreciation potential, optimising risk-adjusted returns.

Sector characteristics heavily influence income profiles. Healthcare REITs, often high-yielding, benefit from demographic trends but face regulatory and operational complexities that impact growth trajectories. Industrial and logistics REITs, currently growth-focused due to e-commerce demand, offer capital appreciation alongside rising income streams. Hospitality REITs exhibit cyclical income variability, requiring nuanced assessment of timing and market exposure. Recognising these sectoral nuances is essential to aligning income strategy with macroeconomic realities.

Real-world case studies illuminate these dynamics. For example, a REIT specialising in senior housing may offer a dependable 5-7%

dividend yield, appealing to retirees seeking reliable income, but may deliver modest capital gains due to the sector's stability and regulatory constraints. Conversely, a data centre REIT might yield 3-4%, reinvesting significant earnings into expanding capacity, thereby achieving substantial capital growth over several years. Investors must evaluate these trade-offs in the context of portfolio objectives and liquidity needs.

Dividend sustainability analysis is paramount. Metrics such as Funds from Operations (FFO) and Adjusted Funds from Operations (AFFO) provide insight into a REIT's capacity to maintain dividends relative to cash flow. Excessive payout ratios above these measures may indicate risk of dividend cuts, while conservative ratios suggest room for growth or resilience during downturns. Transparency in financial reporting enables investors to assess these indicators rigorously, informing more sophisticated income evaluation.

Tax considerations further complicate income profile choices. Dividends from REITs often receive different tax treatment than qualified dividends from equities, potentially affecting net income. Tax-advantaged accounts can mitigate these effects, influencing allocation decisions between high-yield and growth REITs based on investor-specific tax circumstances.

Market conditions and interest rate environments also impact the attractiveness of different income profiles. Rising rates may pressure high-yield REIT valuations as investors seek alternatives with better risk-adjusted returns. Growth REITs, with lower current yields but higher growth potential, might outperform in such scenarios. Conversely, in low-rate environments, stable high-yield REITs become more appealing for income generation. Navigating these cyclical influences demands ongoing portfolio calibration and strategic flexibility.

The evolution of REITs continues to blur traditional distinctions between income and growth. Some REITs adopt hybrid models, balancing dividend distributions with selective reinvestment to capture growth while maintaining income stability. Innovation in property sectors and financing structures further expands the toolkit available to REIT managers, enabling tailored approaches responsive to investor demand and market opportunities.

In synthesising these perspectives, investors are encouraged to approach REIT income profiles with a blend of quantitative analysis, sector understanding, and alignment with personal financial goals. The dichotomy of high yield versus growth is a starting point for deeper engagement with the specific attributes and trajectories of individual REITs and sectors. Mastery of this domain empowers investors to craft portfolios that not only deliver income but also build enduring wealth through informed, strategic participation in real estate markets.

Specialty REITs: Betting on the Future

In the evolving landscape of real estate investment, a subset of Real Estate Investment Trusts (REITs) is pushing the boundaries of traditional property ownership and income generation. Specialty REITs—focused on emerging sectors such as green infrastructure, technology-driven assets, and the rapidly developing cannabis industry—represent a frontier of opportunity and risk that challenges conventional investing paradigms. These REITs are not merely niche players but signal a broader shift in how real estate intersects with innovation, sustainability, and changing social norms. For the discerning investor, understanding the dynamics of specialty REITs is essential to positioning portfolios for future growth while navigating novel complexities.

Green REITs epitomise the convergence of environmental stewardship and real estate finance. They invest in energy-efficient buildings, renewable energy facilities, and sustainable infrastructure designed to reduce carbon footprints and comply with increasingly stringent environmental regulations. The global imperative to combat climate change has accelerated demand for properties that meet green standards, supported by governmental incentives and evolving tenant preferences. These REITs offer exposure to a sector where sustainability is a value driver, not just a compliance cost. Investors should recognise that green REITs often command premium valuations, reflecting long-term operational savings, enhanced asset longevity, and reputational benefits. However, they also face challenges including higher upfront capital expenditures, evolving regulatory frameworks, and the need for continual technological adaptation.

Technology infrastructure REITs occupy another rapidly expanding niche, underpinning the digital economy's backbone. Assets such as cell towers, fibre optic networks, data centres, and satellite facilities are critical to connectivity, cloud computing, and emerging technologies like 5G and edge computing. The explosion of data consumption and reliance on seamless digital infrastructure creates robust demand for these specialised properties. Unlike traditional real estate, these assets often derive value from technology trends and tenant innovation cycles, introducing a unique risk-return profile. Investors must evaluate not only property fundamentals but also technological obsolescence risks, tenant credit quality, and regulatory developments related to data privacy and telecommunications. The growth potential is substantial, but so is the complexity.

The cannabis sector, though nascent and heavily regulated, presents a provocative frontier for specialty REITs. With legalisation spreading across multiple jurisdictions, real estate tailored to cultivation, processing, and retail of cannabis products has become an asset class unto itself. Cannabis REITs typically own specialised industrial properties, including greenhouses and controlled environment facilities, designed to meet stringent regulatory and operational standards. The sector's rapid growth and evolving legal landscape create both opportunities for outsized returns and significant uncertainties. Investors must grapple with regulatory volatility, banking restrictions, and market saturation risks. While early entrants have benefited from first-mover advantages, the path forward demands vigilance, adaptability, and a willingness to engage with an unconventional real estate domain.

These specialty REIT sectors share a common thread: they operate at the intersection of real estate and broader societal transformations. Unlike traditional property classes anchored primarily in physical location and tenant leases, specialty REITs are deeply influenced by technological innovation, regulatory change, and shifting cultural attitudes. This complexity requires investors to augment traditional real estate analysis with sector-specific expertise, trend forecasting, and scenario planning. The integration of financial and thematic factors enriches investment decision-making but also raises the bar for due diligence.

Moreover, specialty REITs often exhibit characteristics akin to startup ventures within the real estate ecosystem. Their business models frequently entail higher growth potential paired with elevated risk, driven by sector uncertainty, rapid innovation cycles, and regulatory flux. Capital deployment strategies may focus on development, acquisitions in emerging markets, or technological upgrades rather than merely managing existing assets. This entrepreneurial approach contrasts with the steady income generation and conservative management of traditional REITs, demanding different investor expectations and risk tolerance.

The evolving landscape of specialty REITs also invites ethical reflection. Investing in green infrastructure aligns with growing emphasis on environmental, social, and governance (ESG) principles, enabling capital to support sustainable development goals. Conversely, cannabis real estate raises questions about social impact, regulatory compliance, and community relations, underscoring the need for responsible investment frameworks. Technology infrastructure REITs grapple with issues of data security, digital equity, and environmental footprints of energy-intensive operations. These considerations amplify the importance of integrating financial analysis with ethical and societal dimensions.

Real-world examples highlight these sectors' potential and pitfalls. A green REIT focused on LEED-certified commercial buildings may deliver stable income while contributing to carbon reduction targets, attracting ESG-conscious investors and premium tenants. A data centre REIT investing in hyperscale facilities for cloud service providers can generate rapid growth but faces substantial capital expenditure and technological risk. Cannabis REITs, pioneering specialised cultivation facilities in regulated states, offer high yield but must navigate complex legal frameworks and market unpredictability. These cases illustrate the heterogeneity and sophistication demanded by specialty REIT investment.

For investors contemplating specialty REITs, portfolio integration requires balancing thematic conviction with traditional diversification principles. Specialty sectors can enhance returns and reduce correlation to conventional real estate, but concentration risk and volatility necessitate judicious allocation. Monitoring sector developments, regulatory changes, and technological advancements is vital to maintaining alignment with investment objectives. Engaging with sector specialists and leveraging data-driven insights further supports effective risk management.

In summary, specialty REITs represent a dynamic and multifaceted frontier in real estate investing. They encapsulate the interplay of innovation, sustainability, and regulatory evolution that is reshaping the asset class. By deepening understanding of green infrastructure, technology assets, and cannabis real estate, investors equip themselves to identify emergent opportunities and manage novel risks. This specialized knowledge is not merely advantageous but indispensable for those seeking to bet thoughtfully on the future of real estate wealth creation.

When REITs Behave Like Startups

The conventional image of a Real Estate Investment Trust (REIT) is that of a stable, dividend-paying enterprise rooted in tangible assets—office buildings, shopping centres, apartment complexes—managed with a conservative, long-term focus. Yet, beneath this traditional façade, an emerging class of REITs operates with an entrepreneurial spirit and growth-oriented ambition more commonly associated with startups than with typical real estate companies. These REITs inhabit high-growth, high-risk environments where agility, innovation, and strategic boldness are paramount. Understanding how these REITs blend the solidity of real estate with the dynamism of startup culture offers a nuanced perspective on real estate investing's evolving frontier.

At first glance, the juxtaposition of REITs and startups might appear paradoxical. Startups are defined by rapid iteration, disruptive innovation, uncertain trajectories, and often volatile funding cycles. REITs, by contrast, are anchored in physical properties and subject to stringent regulatory frameworks mandating income distribution and governance. However, certain REITs defy this dichotomy by embracing strategies that prioritise growth through aggressive acquisitions, development projects, entry into emerging sectors, or pioneering new real estate business models. They deploy capital with a venture-like mindset, accepting elevated risk in pursuit of outsized returns—a bold approach that requires both operational dexterity and financial discipline.

One illustrative example lies in REITs focused on technology infrastructure—data centres, cell towers, fibre networks—assets integral to the digital economy yet subject to rapid technological change and shifting demand patterns. These REITs often reinvest earnings to expand capacity, upgrade facilities, or enter emerging markets, mirroring the scaling ambitions of startups. Their growth depends not only on real estate fundamentals but on technological adoption cycles, tenant innovation, and regulatory environments, introducing layers of complexity uncommon in traditional property sectors. Investors must therefore evaluate these REITs not just as real estate managers but as active participants in technology-driven markets.

Similarly, REITs involved in specialty sectors such as life sciences, cannabis-related properties, or renewable energy infrastructure display entrepreneurial characteristics. These industries are often nascent, regulated, and evolving, requiring REIT managers to develop sector-specific expertise, cultivate strategic partnerships, and navigate uncertainty. The pace of change in these sectors necessitates flexible capital deployment and a willingness to pivot—traits emblematic of startup ventures. This operational approach contrasts with the buy-and-hold mentality prevalent in classic real estate investing, signaling a hybrid model where asset ownership intersects with innovation and risk-taking.

Development-focused REITs further exemplify this blend. Engaging in ground-up construction or substantial redevelopment projects entails greater execution risk, longer timelines, and capital intensity than acquiring stabilized assets. Yet, successful development can unlock significant value and growth, akin to a startup's product launch or market expansion. These REITs often cultivate entrepreneurial cultures within their organisations, incentivising innovation, agility, and responsiveness to market signals. They operate with heightened sensitivity to financing costs, regulatory approvals, and market demand forecasts, navigating a complex project ecosystem that demands both real estate acumen and startup-like adaptability.

This convergence of REITs and startup dynamics also reshapes investor experience and expectations. Investors in growth-oriented REITs must reconcile the income-focused framework of traditional trusts with the higher volatility and capital reinvestment patterns typical of startup ventures. Dividends may be lower or more variable, reflecting retained earnings and development costs. Share price fluctuations can be more pronounced, driven by growth prospects and execution risks rather than solely income stability. This profile appeals to investors with longer horizons, tolerance for risk, and appetite for innovation-led returns, diverging from the conservative, income-centric investor archetype.

Critically, governance and risk management remain foundational in these hybrid REITs. While entrepreneurial in spirit, they operate under regulatory scrutiny that imposes discipline and transparency. Boards oversee management with a focus on balancing growth ambitions against fiduciary responsibilities, ensuring capital allocation aligns with shareholder interests and risk tolerance. This governance structure differentiates them from pure startups, anchoring growth strategies in accountability and regulatory compliance. The interplay between innovation and oversight defines a unique governance challenge and opportunity.

The entrepreneurial approach adopted by these REITs reflects broader economic and technological shifts reshaping real estate demand and value creation. Urbanisation, digitisation, climate change, and evolving consumer preferences create dynamic market conditions that reward agility and innovation. REITs that adapt by integrating startup methodologies—rapid iteration, market responsiveness, strategic partnerships—position themselves to capture emerging value streams unavailable to traditional models. This transformation elevates the role of real estate from passive asset to active business platform, redefining what it means to invest in property.

From an investor's perspective, recognising when REITs behave like startups informs portfolio construction and risk management. Such REITs complement stable, income-generating assets by adding growth potential and diversification. They also necessitate enhanced due diligence—examining management track records, sector knowledge, capital strategy, and operational execution capacity. Understanding the distinct risk-return profile of these REITs enables investors to calibrate exposure consistent with financial goals and risk appetite.

In essence, the intersection of REITs and startup culture represents a frontier in real estate investment, blending tangible asset ownership with entrepreneurial drive and innovation. This hybrid model challenges traditional categorizations, demanding new analytical frameworks and investor mindsets. For those willing to engage deeply, it offers pathways to dynamic growth, sector leadership, and portfolio differentiation—hallmarks of the next evolution in real estate wealth creation.

Chapter 5
Public vs. Private REITs—The Visibility Dilemma

In the intricate world of real estate investment trusts, one of the most consequential choices an investor faces is the decision between public and private REITs—a choice imbued with both promise and peril. At its heart lies a tension between transparency, liquidity, and market efficiency on one hand, and the allure of exclusivity, potentially superior returns, and access to unique assets on the other. This chapter confronts the visibility dilemma, exploring the differences between investing in public markets, where information is abundant and timely, and the more opaque realm of private REITs. Successfully navigating this divide requires careful analysis, disciplined due diligence, and a clear understanding of how visibility—both literal and figurative—affects outcomes.

Public REITs epitomise openness and accessibility. Traded on major stock exchanges and subject to stringent regulatory oversight, they offer investors real-time pricing, liquidity, and comprehensive disclosures. Shareholders can monitor portfolio composition, dividend policies, leverage, and operational metrics with relative ease. The dual forces of market scrutiny and regulatory compliance establish governance standards and investor protections that are difficult to replicate elsewhere. Yet this transparency is not without trade-offs: public REITs are vulnerable to market sentiment, short-term volatility, and the pressures of quarterly reporting, which can incentivise management to prioritise immediate results over long-term value creation. Investors gain liquidity and clarity, but they cede some control over timing and strategic manoeuvres.

Private REITs, by contrast, inhabit a far less visible space, offering access to specialised real estate opportunities often absent from public markets. These vehicles may target niche sectors, bespoke developments, or illiquid assets, promising potentially enhanced yields and diversification. Their exclusivity appeals to high-net-worth individuals and institutional investors seeking discretion and tailored strategies. Yet the opacity inherent in private REITs conceals critical information: valuations are infrequent and subjective, liquidity is limited, and reporting standards can be inconsistent. Such obscurity can mask underlying risks, inflate performance metrics, or obscure conflicts of interest, posing substantial challenges to informed decision-making and investor protection.

The attraction of private REITs—the promise of differentiated assets, outsized returns, and limited competition—must be weighed carefully against these risks. Investors encounter high entry thresholds, lock-up periods, and scarce secondary markets. Ambiguities in valuation complicate assessments of portfolio health and exit timing. History offers cautionary tales: during the 2008 financial crisis, private real estate vehicles faced severe liquidity constraints, leaving investors exposed to extended capital lock-ups and significant markdowns. The lesson is evident: the absence of visibility can turn potential into speculation, requiring a disciplined, sceptical approach.

Robust due diligence is indispensable in navigating private REITs. Investors must critically evaluate governance structures, appraisal methodologies, fee arrangements, and sponsor track records. Warning signs include opaque reporting, inconsistent valuations, excessive leverage, and misaligned incentives. Engaging third-party auditors, legal counsel, and industry specialists is crucial for peeling back layers of complexity and verifying claims. Far from a perfunctory exercise, due diligence in private REITs demands sustained attention, analytical rigour, and a healthy dose of scepticism.

Prioritising transparency over allure entails valuing clarity, alignment, and accountability above exclusivity or marketing gloss. Public REITs, with their regulated structures and transparent pricing, offer a foundation for confidence and liquidity management. Private REITs can complement portfolios by providing exposure to unconventional assets, but such access must be approached judiciously, through thoroughly vetted channels. Investors who foreground structural soundness and transparency position themselves to engage the real estate landscape with informed conviction rather than speculative optimism.

This chapter unpacks the structural, operational, and psychological dimensions of public versus private REIT investing. By examining the advantages and limitations of each, and providing practical frameworks for evaluation, it moves beyond binary thinking to a nuanced understanding of how visibility shapes risk, return, and investment success. Appreciating this visibility dilemma is not a theoretical exercise—it is a practical necessity in a market where real estate's promise rests as much on clarity and trust as it does on the assets themselves. Through this lens, investors are encouraged to question assumptions, refine strategies, and approach wealth creation in real estate with the disciplined insight demanded by contemporary markets.

What You See Is What You Get?

Investing in public Real Estate Investment Trusts (REITs) offers an experience that is, in many respects, transparent and immediate: market prices fluctuate openly, financial statements are readily accessible, and trading liquidity affords investors the freedom to enter or exit positions with relative ease. This clarity and accessibility are among the chief advantages that distinguish public REITs from their private counterparts, making them a preferred vehicle for many seeking real estate exposure without the complications of direct ownership. Yet, the visible surface of public REIT investing belies a series of trade-offs—some subtle, others profound—that investors must understand to navigate this space wisely and align their expectations with the realities of public market dynamics.

Liquidity stands as perhaps the most compelling benefit of public REITs. Unlike private real estate investments, where capital is typically locked in for extended periods and secondary markets are often illiquid or opaque, public REIT shares trade on major stock exchanges with daily volume and transparent pricing. This liquidity not only facilitates portfolio flexibility but also empowers investors to respond swiftly to changing market conditions, personal financial needs, or strategic realignments. The ability to buy or sell shares with minimal delay enhances risk management and enables tactical asset allocation—qualities highly prized in dynamic investment environments.

Complementing liquidity is the hallmark of transparency intrinsic to public REITs. Regulatory regimes governing public companies impose rigorous disclosure requirements, including quarterly and annual financial reports, management discussions, risk assessments, and governance disclosures. Investors benefit from a wealth of data—earnings metrics, funds from operations (FFO), debt levels, occupancy rates, lease maturities, and more—allowing for granular analysis of performance drivers and risk exposures. This transparency not only facilitates due diligence but also fosters market discipline, as management teams are held accountable by shareholders, analysts, and regulators alike. The comprehensive information ecosystem supports informed decision-making and reduces asymmetries that can plague less visible investment vehicles.

Market pricing further enriches the public REIT proposition. Share prices reflect the collective judgments of myriad market participants, integrating real-time information, macroeconomic trends, sector developments, and sentiment. This price discovery mechanism offers investors a continuous gauge of value, enabling timely assessment of entry and exit points. While market prices can exhibit volatility, they also embed expectations about growth prospects, risk, and competitive positioning—factors essential for active portfolio management. Access to this transparent pricing contrasts sharply with private REITs, where valuations may rely on infrequent appraisals or sponsor estimates, often detached from current market realities.

However, these benefits are not without cost. Public REIT investors trade off certain advantages for liquidity and transparency. Market exposure subjects REIT shares to the whims of equity markets, including volatility driven by macroeconomic shifts, interest rate changes, geopolitical events, and investor sentiment—factors that may have limited impact on underlying property fundamentals. This disconnect can result in share price swings that obscure asset quality or long-term value, challenging investors to maintain discipline and focus beyond short-term noise.

Furthermore, the regulatory and public nature of listed REITs imposes constraints on management strategy. Quarterly reporting pressures can encourage a focus on short-term earnings and dividend stability, potentially at the expense of opportunistic investments or long-term innovation. Public scrutiny may also limit flexibility in capital structure adjustments or strategic pivots. These dynamics contrast with private REITs' relative freedom to pursue bespoke strategies away from public markets' spotlight, albeit at the expense of transparency and liquidity.

Public REITs also confront competitive market forces that can compress yields and elevate valuation multiples, particularly during periods of strong investor demand for real estate securities. This can challenge income-focused investors seeking attractive dividend returns, requiring careful sector and security selection to balance yield and growth. Understanding valuation metrics in the context of interest rates, economic cycles, and sector fundamentals becomes imperative to avoid overpaying for perceived transparency.

Examining real-world examples highlights these dynamics. For instance, public retail REITs have seen share price volatility reflecting changing consumer behaviours and pandemic disruptions, despite stable underlying lease agreements in many cases. Conversely, industrial REITs enjoying e-commerce tailwinds have attracted premium valuations, requiring investors to assess sustainability amid rising capital costs. These sectoral variations underscore that visibility and liquidity do not eliminate risk or complexity but provide tools to manage them with insight.

Investors must also appreciate the role of market sentiment and behavioural biases within public REIT investing. Herd behaviour, momentum trading, and macro fears can exaggerate price moves, occasionally decoupling shares from fundamental values. Thus, public REIT ownership demands a disciplined approach grounded in rigorous analysis, valuation acumen, and patience. The readily available information can be both a boon and a challenge, necessitating skillful navigation.

In essence, the maxim "what you see is what you get" encapsulates the dual-edged nature of public REIT investing. Visibility through liquidity, transparency, and market pricing equips investors with clarity and control unseen in many alternative real estate vehicles. Yet, these very attributes expose investors to market forces, short-termism, and valuation dynamics requiring sophisticated understanding and strategy. Recognising and balancing these trade-offs is central to leveraging public REITs effectively within diversified portfolios.

This nuanced perspective enables investors to move beyond superficial attraction to liquidity or transparency alone, towards a comprehensive grasp of how these features influence risk, return, and portfolio resilience. The clarity of public markets, when combined with disciplined analysis and strategic intent, empowers investors to capture real estate's economic benefits while managing the inherent uncertainties of market participation.

Private REITs: Rich in Promise, Opaque in Practice

The allure of private Real Estate Investment Trusts (REITs) lies in their promise to unlock unique real estate opportunities often unavailable through public markets. Offering access to niche properties, bespoke strategies, and potentially higher yields, private REITs attract institutional investors and high-net-worth individuals seeking portfolio diversification beyond traditional avenues. However, beneath this promise lies a landscape marked by complexity, opacity, and considerable risks that require a discerning eye and rigorous scrutiny. Understanding the structural nuances, liquidity constraints, and valuation ambiguities inherent in private REITs is essential for any investor contemplating participation in this less visible segment of real estate investment.

At their core, private REITs operate outside the scrutiny and regulation imposed on their publicly traded counterparts. This exemption permits greater flexibility in investment mandates, asset selection, and operational strategies, allowing managers to pursue illiquid or specialised assets that may offer superior risk-adjusted returns. Examples include private commercial developments, senior housing, self-storage portfolios, or industrial complexes not typically accessible through public channels. Such offerings can provide enhanced income profiles or capital appreciation potential, making private REITs an attractive complement to public real estate holdings.

Yet, this very flexibility comes at the cost of transparency. Unlike public REITs, private vehicles are not obligated to disclose detailed financial reports, market valuations, or governance practices in a timely and standardised manner. Investors often rely on periodic, sponsor-generated reports which may lack comparability and depth, impeding the ability to perform thorough due diligence. Valuation methodologies in private REITs frequently depend on appraisals conducted at intervals rather than continuous market pricing, introducing subjectivity and potential mispricing. This opacity can obscure true portfolio health, risk exposures, and the sustainability of distributions.

Liquidity is another fundamental challenge. Private REIT investments typically entail capital lock-ups extending several years, limiting investors' ability to redeem shares or exit positions in response to market changes or personal needs. Secondary markets for private REIT shares, where they exist, are often thin and inefficient, potentially forcing sales at significant discounts. This illiquidity contrasts starkly with the daily tradability of public REIT shares and introduces a layer of risk that must be factored into asset allocation decisions. Investors must reconcile their liquidity requirements with the inherent constraints of private real estate investing.

Access barriers further complicate private REIT participation. Minimum investment thresholds, often substantial, restrict these opportunities to accredited investors or institutions. The complexity and resource intensity of evaluating private offerings also limit accessibility, demanding specialised expertise and due diligence capabilities often beyond the reach of individual investors. Consequently, private REITs remain an exclusive domain, with participation contingent on both capital and knowledge, raising questions about democratization and equitable access within real estate finance.

Historical and contemporary case studies underscore these tensions. During the 2008 financial crisis, many private real estate funds faced severe liquidity squeezes and valuation write-downs, revealing vulnerabilities obscured by infrequent reporting and limited market transparency. More recently, certain private REITs targeting emerging sectors have grappled with operational challenges and regulatory shifts, testing the resilience and adaptability of their strategies. These episodes highlight the potential for both significant reward and pronounced risk, demanding vigilant oversight and investor scepticism.

Due diligence in private REIT investing transcends standard checklist exercises; it requires deep engagement with sponsor credibility, governance structures, fee arrangements, asset quality, leverage levels, and exit strategies. Investors must interrogate valuation processes, scrutinise historical performance in various market conditions, and assess alignment of interests between sponsors and shareholders. Red flags include opaque fee structures, lack of independent oversight, inconsistent reporting, and overly optimistic projections. Engaging third-party advisors, legal counsel, and industry specialists enhances the robustness of due diligence and mitigates informational asymmetries.

Ethical considerations also surface in private REITs, particularly concerning transparency and investor protection. The balance between proprietary strategy confidentiality and the fiduciary duty to disclose material information is delicate. Sponsors must navigate these responsibilities conscientiously to foster trust and maintain reputational capital. Investors, in turn, bear the onus of demanding transparency and accountability, recognising that exclusivity should not equate to diminished governance standards.

Portfolio integration of private REITs demands strategic calibration. While these vehicles can enhance diversification and yield, their illiquidity and opacity necessitate appropriate sizing within broader portfolios. Investors should view private REITs as complementing, rather than replacing, public real estate exposure, leveraging their unique attributes while managing concentration and liquidity risks. Ongoing monitoring and re-assessment are essential to respond to evolving market conditions and asset performance.

In essence, private REITs encapsulate a paradox of promise and opacity. Their capacity to deliver differentiated real estate exposure and potential enhanced returns is counterbalanced by challenges in transparency, liquidity, and access. For investors equipped with rigorous due diligence processes, specialised expertise, and a clear-eyed understanding of risks, private REITs can constitute a valuable component of a sophisticated real estate portfolio. However, this domain demands caution, discipline, and an unwavering commitment to informed, critical evaluation—qualities that distinguish prudent participation from speculative enthusiasm.

Due Diligence or Wishful Thinking?

Investing in non-public Real Estate Investment Trusts (REITs) demands a degree of caution and analytical rigor that far exceeds the approach typical of publicly traded securities. The opacity and complexity surrounding these private offerings create fertile ground not only for genuine opportunity but also for misplaced optimism and costly misjudgments. The critical question investors must ask themselves is whether their assessment rests on disciplined due diligence or on hopeful assumptions glossed over by persuasive marketing. Developing a robust framework for evaluating private REITs is essential to separating prudent investment from wishful thinking, preserving capital while positioning portfolios to benefit from carefully vetted growth prospects.

Private REITs, by design, offer limited disclosure and operate in less regulated environments compared to their public counterparts. This lack of transparency necessitates a more proactive and skeptical approach from investors. It is not enough to accept sponsor-provided summaries or glossy presentations at face value; the onus lies with the investor to interrogate underlying assumptions, validate claims, and probe areas prone to obfuscation. Effective due diligence in this context functions as a defensive mechanism, safeguarding against incomplete information, conflicts of interest, and overly optimistic projections that may distort risk perception.

Central to this process is a mental checklist grounded in critical inquiry. Investors should begin by scrutinising the sponsor's track record: past performance, alignment of interests, and governance practices. A sponsor with a demonstrated history of delivering consistent returns and transparent communication provides a foundational layer of credibility. Equally important is the structure of the REIT itself, including fee arrangements, distribution policies, and liquidity provisions. High fees or complex distribution waterfalls can erode investor returns, while restrictive redemption terms can trap capital during adverse market conditions. Understanding these structural features in detail equips investors to assess net economic benefit realistically.

Valuation methodologies merit particular attention. Unlike public REITs, private offerings seldom benefit from market-driven price discovery, relying instead on periodic appraisals that incorporate subjective judgements and may lag current market conditions. Investors must evaluate the frequency, independence, and methodology of valuations, probing for signs of inflated asset values or smoothing of performance metrics. Cross-referencing valuations against comparable market transactions and sector trends helps anchor expectations in empirical reality rather than promotional narrative.

Operational due diligence involves a close examination of portfolio composition, tenant quality, lease terms, and geographic diversification. Investors should seek clarity on occupancy rates, tenant concentration risks, and lease maturity schedules to gauge income stability and vulnerability to economic cycles. A well-diversified portfolio with creditworthy tenants and staggered lease expirations suggests resilience, while overreliance on a narrow tenant base or market segment signals concentration risk. Physical asset condition and capital expenditure requirements also affect long-term value preservation, underscoring the need for detailed property-level analysis.

Risk management practices employed by the REIT and its sponsor are another critical focus area. How does the REIT manage leverage, market risk, and operational contingencies? Are there robust mechanisms for monitoring and mitigating risks inherent in property management, financing, and regulatory compliance? A lax approach to risk control may foreshadow heightened vulnerability during economic downturns or sector-specific shocks. Investors benefit from seeking evidence of proactive risk governance, including transparent reporting of stress testing, scenario analysis, and contingency planning.

Red flags abound in the private REIT landscape and demand vigilance. Overly optimistic projected returns without commensurate explanation, lack of independent audits, absence of third-party legal review, and unusually restrictive investor rights should prompt caution. Sponsors who resist or obfuscate information requests undermine investor confidence and elevate uncertainty. Similarly, aggressive use of leverage, inconsistent financial reporting, or changes in key personnel without clear communication can signal deeper issues. Identifying these warning signs early is critical to avoiding costly missteps.

Psychological factors also influence private REIT investment decisions. The appeal of exclusivity, fear of missing out, and trust in charismatic sponsors can cloud judgement, leading investors to overlook red flags or underappreciate risks. Cultivating a mindset grounded in skepticism, discipline, and methodical analysis helps counteract these biases. Engaging independent advisors, seeking peer perspectives, and conducting scenario-based stress testing further enhance decision quality.

Real-world cases illustrate the consequences of due diligence failures and successes. Instances where private real estate vehicles faltered under market stress often trace back to insufficient transparency and overreliance on sponsor assurances. Conversely, investors who performed exhaustive diligence, demanded rigorous disclosures, and maintained adaptive monitoring were better positioned to weather turbulence or identify exit opportunities. These lessons affirm that diligence is not a one-time act but an ongoing commitment essential to safeguarding capital and optimising returns.

Ultimately, distinguishing due diligence from wishful thinking transforms private REIT investing from speculation to informed participation. The comprehensive evaluation of sponsor credibility, structural terms, valuation integrity, operational soundness, risk governance, and red flags constructs a robust decision framework. This framework enables investors to navigate the inherent opacity and complexity of private REITs with clarity and confidence, aligning capital allocation with realistic assessments of risk and reward.

Embracing such rigor respects the unique challenges of non-public real estate investing, honours fiduciary responsibility, and positions investors to capitalise on genuine opportunities without succumbing to the allure of unchecked optimism. This disciplined approach serves as a vital compass amid the uncertainties and promises that define the private REIT terrain.

Choosing Visibility Over Hype

In the complex world of real estate investment, where opportunity often intersects with ambiguity, the allure of exclusivity and polished marketing can easily cloud judgment. Private Real Estate Investment Trusts (REITs), by their very nature, offer a seductive promise: access to lucrative assets unavailable to the general public, the potential for outsized returns, and the prestige of being part of an elite investment circle. Yet, beneath the surface of carefully crafted presentations and selective disclosures lies a crucial question—should investors prioritise visibility, clarity, and alignment over hype and exclusivity? This article argues emphatically that transparency and strategic fit serve as far superior filters for real estate investments than marketing gloss or perceived scarcity.

Visibility in investment is not merely about data availability; it encompasses the quality, frequency, and reliability of information that enables investors to assess risks and rewards with confidence. Public REITs exemplify this principle, offering continuous market pricing, detailed financial disclosures, and regulatory oversight that collectively empower investors to make informed decisions. The market's pricing mechanism reflects collective intelligence and real-time adjustments, reducing informational asymmetry and enhancing accountability. This openness contrasts starkly with the opaque nature of many private REITs, where limited reporting, infrequent valuations, and restricted investor access obscure true performance and risk profiles.

Exclusivity, while often marketed as a virtue, can act as a double-edged sword. Private REITs frequently leverage the perception of scarcity to justify high fees, limited liquidity, and reduced transparency. This cultivated aura can disarm investor skepticism, prompting decisions driven by fear of missing out rather than grounded analysis. In reality, exclusivity without visibility amplifies uncertainty, undermining the very foundation of prudent investing. A well-known example is the surge of private real estate funds prior to the 2008 financial crisis, where limited investor access and opaque valuations contributed to protracted liquidity crunches and unexpected losses. Such historical lessons underscore the dangers of conflating exclusivity with quality.

Marketing polish compounds this risk. Professional presentations, compelling narratives, and confident projections can obscure structural weaknesses, misaligned incentives, or inflated return expectations. Skilled sponsors craft stories that resonate emotionally and intellectually, but these narratives must be interrogated critically. Investors should prioritise substance over style, demanding evidence of consistent performance, robust governance, and alignment of interests rather than succumbing to glossy appeal. The temptation to equate polished marketing with assured success remains a persistent hazard in private real estate investing.

Alignment of interests emerges as a pivotal criterion for discerning investors. Visibility enables scrutiny of fee structures, distribution policies, and sponsor equity stakes, illuminating whether managers' incentives truly align with those of investors. Transparent vehicles often feature clear governance mechanisms, independent boards, and disclosure practices that safeguard shareholder value. Conversely, opaque private REITs may obscure fee complexities, promote excessive leverage, or incentivise growth at the expense of capital preservation. Prioritising alignment over exclusivity mitigates agency risks and fosters sustainable investment relationships.

Strategic fit constitutes another essential dimension of visibility's value. Investments should be evaluated within the context of the investor's overall portfolio objectives, liquidity needs, risk tolerance, and time horizon. Transparent information facilitates accurate assessment of how a given REIT complements or diversifies existing holdings. Exclusive offerings, by contrast, may lack the clarity necessary to gauge their role or to execute effective portfolio construction. Investors benefit from frameworks that integrate visibility into asset allocation decisions rather than chasing allure without measurable fit.

The behavioural dimension also warrants attention. Investors operating in environments characterised by opacity and exclusivity may experience cognitive biases—overconfidence, anchoring, or herd mentality—that skew judgment. Visibility acts as an antidote, anchoring decisions in verifiable facts and measurable performance rather than in emotion or hype. Cultivating a culture of disciplined inquiry and scepticism enables investors to resist seductive narratives and maintain focus on long-term value creation.

Practical application of these principles demands rigorous due diligence processes tailored to the visibility challenge. Investors should insist on regular, detailed reporting, independent audits, and transparent valuation methodologies. Engagement with sponsors should be proactive, seeking clarifications and challenging assumptions. When information gaps persist or disclosures lack substance, the prudent course is caution, recognising that the absence of visibility is itself a significant risk factor.

Real-world examples reinforce the primacy of visibility. REITs that maintain robust disclosure practices, clear governance, and open communication tend to engender investor trust, attract broader capital bases, and demonstrate resilience across market cycles. Conversely, those that rely heavily on exclusivity and marketing often face heightened scrutiny, legal challenges, or reputational damage when underlying issues surface. These patterns affirm that visibility is not merely a regulatory requirement but a strategic asset that underpins long-term success.

In sum, choosing visibility over hype is a decisive act of investment discipline. It acknowledges that sustainable real estate investing rests on transparency, alignment, and clarity rather than on mystique or marketing flair. Investors who embrace this philosophy position themselves to navigate complexity with confidence, make reasoned decisions, and build portfolios resilient to both market fluctuations and behavioural pitfalls. Visibility empowers not just insight but also integrity, setting the foundation for real estate wealth creation that is both informed and enduring.

Chapter 6
Getting Started—Opening Your REIT Investment Life

Embarking on the journey of REIT investing often stirs a mixture of anticipation and trepidation, particularly for those encountering this distinctive asset class for the first time. The allure is undeniable: the potential for steady income, portfolio diversification, and long-term growth. Yet, the initial steps can feel perplexing. Where does one even start? Which platforms or accounts are appropriate? And how does one discern suitable REITs or funds? This chapter seeks to strip away that uncertainty, offering a clear roadmap to transform hesitation into confident, informed action.

For many newcomers, the first hurdle is logistical: setting up the right accounts and understanding how to gain access. Today's investment landscape has evolved dramatically—online brokerages, discount platforms, and streamlined account structures make entry far more accessible than in decades past. A relatively modest initial commitment, sometimes just a few hundred pounds, can secure exposure to public REITs or REIT ETFs. Navigating the differences between account types—from Individual Savings Accounts (ISAs) and Self-Invested Personal Pensions (SIPPs) to standard brokerage accounts—is essential, given the varied tax treatments and protections on offer. This section provides step-by-step guidance, equipping readers with the confidence to execute their first purchase with foresight and precision.

Once that initial barrier is crossed, attention turns to portfolio construction. Objectives vary widely: some investors seek steady income to supplement retirement, others aim to generate cash flow for ongoing expenses, while many pursue capital growth through diversified sector exposure. Designing a REIT-focused portfolio demands a disciplined approach, balancing income reliability against growth potential. Sector choices—residential, industrial, healthcare, technology infrastructure—respond differently to economic cycles and market trends. Thoughtful alignment of portfolio composition with personal goals, risk tolerance, and investment horizon is critical;

REIT investing is not a one-size-fits-all pursuit, but a spectrum of customised strategies.

Psychological barriers, however, can prove as formidable as financial ones. Fear of market timing, concerns over dividend fluctuations, and anxiety around valuations can stall even experienced investors. This chapter reframes such variability as an intrinsic feature of financial markets rather than a flaw. Strategies such as dollar-cost averaging, focusing on long-term compounding, and interpreting dividend volatility within the context of broader economic cycles help cultivate rational, decisive engagement. By embracing a systematic, patient approach, investors can temper emotional biases and convert market dynamics into strategic advantage.

Importantly, REIT investing should be approached not as a series of isolated transactions, but as a coherent, long-term strategy. Reinvestment plans, disciplined portfolio reviews, and an appreciation of compounding effects transform periodic purchases into an engine of growth. Short-term reactions and speculative behaviour give way to horizon-focused thinking, where consistent contributions and dividend reinvestment generate enduring value. Achieving this demands education, discipline, and a willingness to learn continuously—qualities this chapter endeavours to instil.

Real-world examples punctuate the discussion, bringing abstract concepts into practical focus. Stepwise guides to account setup, comparisons of portfolio allocations for different investor profiles, and analyses of behavioural pitfalls ground theoretical insights in lived experience. Readers are encouraged to reflect on their circumstances and ambitions, translating guidance into personalised, actionable strategies.

Ultimately, this chapter extends beyond the mechanics of REIT investing. It is an invitation to reimagine real estate wealth: to move from ownership defined by deeds and management burdens to a framework measured by income streams, diversification, and disciplined growth. By demystifying entry, addressing apprehensions, and fostering strategic thinking, it transforms what can feel like tentative first steps into a confident stride toward building a resilient, income-oriented real estate portfolio—turning the promise of REITs into tangible financial reality.

The First $500: Where to Begin

Initiating one's investment journey in Real Estate Investment Trusts (REITs) often confronts an initial barrier of uncertainty—questions about where to start, how much capital is necessary, and what practical steps are involved. Contrary to the misconception that real estate investing demands large sums or intricate procedures, today's financial landscape offers accessible entry points that democratise ownership. The reality is that with as little as $500—approximately £400—an investor can acquire meaningful exposure to a diversified real estate portfolio through public REITs or REIT exchange-traded funds (ETFs). This section dispels complexity by methodically outlining how to establish the essential brokerage accounts, select appropriate platforms, and execute the first purchase, empowering readers to transform intention into tangible asset ownership with clarity and confidence.

The foundation of REIT investing begins with understanding account structures and brokerage options. While traditional investment accounts remain available, modern online brokerages have revolutionised accessibility, offering streamlined application processes, competitive fee schedules, and intuitive interfaces tailored to varying investor experience levels. Investors must consider account types—including Individual Savings Accounts (ISAs), Self-Invested Personal Pensions (SIPPs), and standard taxable accounts—as each bears distinct tax implications and regulatory protections. For example, utilizing a Stocks and Shares ISA can shelter dividends and capital gains from UK taxes, enhancing net returns over time. Selecting the appropriate account requires aligning investment goals with tax efficiency and liquidity preferences, a critical early step in establishing a sustainable investment framework.

With account infrastructure in place, platform selection becomes paramount. The market hosts a broad spectrum of brokerages, from full-service firms offering research support to discount platforms prioritising low costs and execution speed. Investors should prioritise platforms with reputable regulatory standing, robust security measures, and transparent fee disclosures. Importantly, the availability of fractional share trading—allowing purchase of partial shares—has lowered capital thresholds, enabling investors to participate in higher-priced REITs or ETFs without full share purchase requirements. Platforms supporting fractional trading thus facilitate diversified portfolio construction even with limited initial capital.

Once the technical prerequisites are satisfied, the focus shifts to selecting the first REIT or REIT ETF. Individual REITs represent shares in companies owning and managing income-producing real estate, offering direct exposure but with inherent company-specific risks. REIT ETFs aggregate multiple REITs, providing instant diversification across sectors and geographies, which can reduce volatility and administrative burdens. The choice depends on investor objectives, risk tolerance, and preference for active versus passive management. For beginners, REIT ETFs often represent a prudent starting point, balancing accessibility with risk mitigation.

Navigating the mechanics of placing the first trade involves understanding order types—market orders execute immediately at prevailing prices, while limit orders specify acceptable price thresholds. Beginners benefit from market orders to ensure execution but should monitor market conditions to avoid unexpected price swings. Recognising trading hours, settlement cycles, and potential brokerage commissions informs cost-effective execution strategies. Practical familiarity with platform interfaces and order confirmations cultivates investor confidence and reduces operational errors.

Beyond the transactional, this initial phase invites investors to frame their entry as a deliberate strategic act rather than an impulsive purchase. The significance of the first $500 lies not in its size but in its role as a foundation for disciplined, incremental portfolio building. Employing dollar-cost averaging—investing fixed amounts periodically regardless of market fluctuations—smooths entry prices and mitigates timing risks. Coupling this with dividend reinvestment strategies compounds wealth over time, transforming modest beginnings into substantial financial footholds.

This foundational investment stage also requires confronting psychological barriers common among new investors: fear of market volatility, concerns about valuation, and hesitation born of perceived complexity. Educational resources, simulated trading environments, and consultation with financial advisors can alleviate anxieties and foster informed decision-making. Emphasising process over perfection empowers investors to prioritise consistent engagement over elusive timing, recognising that early participation and persistence outweigh attempts at market prediction.

Real-world illustrations further contextualise the accessibility of beginning with a modest investment. Consider an investor using a leading UK online brokerage to open a Stocks and Shares ISA, depositing £500 to acquire shares in a broad-based REIT ETF tracking UK and global real estate markets. Over a decade, with dividend reinvestment and additional contributions, this initial outlay can evolve into a diversified, income-generating portfolio reflecting global property cycles. Such cases exemplify how structural access and disciplined strategies translate modest capital into meaningful real estate exposure.

In sum, the first $500 represents more than a monetary threshold; it is the gateway to participating in a complex, evolving asset class with profound implications for wealth creation. Through clear understanding of account setups, platform capabilities, trade mechanics, and strategic frameworks, investors can demystify the initiation process, overcoming inertia and fostering a mindset oriented toward sustainable, long-term real estate investment. This clarity lays the groundwork for informed progression, from initial purchase to comprehensive portfolio management, heralding a new chapter in financial autonomy and opportunity.

Setting Up a REIT-Only Portfolio

Designing a portfolio exclusively composed of Real Estate Investment Trusts (REITs) presents a unique opportunity to harness the income-generating power and diversification benefits of real estate within a liquid, accessible framework. However, this endeavour demands more than assembling a collection of ticker symbols; it requires a nuanced understanding of investor objectives, sector dynamics, risk profiles, and income-growth trade-offs. Whether the goal is to generate reliable retirement income, supplement cash flow, or pursue capital appreciation, constructing a REIT-only portfolio calls for strategic intentionality, balancing individual needs against the complex realities of real estate markets and financial instruments.

An income-centric REIT portfolio prioritises stable, predictable dividend streams, typically appealing to investors seeking to support living expenses, replace salary income, or sustain post-retirement lifestyles. Such portfolios often emphasise REIT sectors characterised by long-term leases, high occupancy, and essential services—healthcare facilities, residential apartments, industrial logistics hubs, and commercial office spaces with creditworthy tenants. Selecting REITs with strong funds from operations (FFO), conservative payout ratios, and demonstrated dividend track records mitigates the risk of payout cuts and income volatility. Sector diversification within this framework remains vital to cushion against cyclical downturns affecting any single property type or geography. For example, healthcare REITs may offer resilience during economic slowdowns, while industrial REITs benefit from e-commerce trends but may face supply chain risks.

Conversely, a growth-oriented REIT portfolio focuses on capital appreciation alongside, or sometimes in lieu of, dividend income. This approach often targets sectors and strategies with higher risk-return profiles: data centre REITs riding the digital infrastructure wave, technology-driven logistics hubs, or specialty REITs investing in emerging asset classes such as life sciences or renewable energy facilities. These REITs may retain earnings to fund expansion, resulting in lower immediate yields but greater potential for share price appreciation. Investors adopting this strategy must exhibit tolerance for sector-specific volatility and a longer investment horizon, recognising that growth-oriented portfolios can complement traditional income streams and enhance total return over time.

Many investors seek a hybrid strategy, blending income reliability with growth potential to achieve balanced risk-adjusted returns. Constructing such a portfolio involves allocating capital across diverse REIT sectors, balancing high-yield, stable dividend payers with innovative, growth-focused trusts. Asset allocation decisions hinge on personal circumstances, including age, liquidity needs, tax considerations, and broader portfolio composition. Regular portfolio rebalancing ensures alignment with evolving goals and market conditions, preventing unintended sector concentration or risk drift.

Geographical diversification further enhances portfolio resilience. While domestic REITs may provide familiarity and regulatory comfort, international REITs offer exposure to markets with distinct economic drivers, currency effects, and demographic trends. European healthcare REITs, Asian logistics trusts, or Australian residential REITs, for instance, contribute unique risk-return characteristics. However, investing globally introduces complexities—foreign exchange risk, differing accounting standards, and regulatory environments—that must be carefully assessed and managed.

The selection process benefits from rigorous fundamental analysis combined with macroeconomic context. Evaluating a REIT's management quality, balance sheet strength, growth pipeline, and tenant quality is as crucial as understanding interest rate sensitivity and inflation exposure inherent in real estate assets. For example, REITs with variable lease structures may hedge inflation risk better than those with fixed rents, an important consideration amid fluctuating price levels. Investors should also appraise governance practices and transparency, which influence long-term performance and risk mitigation.

Technology has transformed portfolio construction and management, with digital tools enabling sophisticated screening, backtesting, and ongoing monitoring of REIT holdings. Platforms offering real-time data, analyst reports, and automated alerts empower investors to respond promptly to market shifts, dividend changes, or sectoral developments. Yet, technology complements rather than replaces critical thinking; investors must interpret data judiciously within strategic frameworks rather than react reflexively to transient fluctuations.

Behavioral considerations merit emphasis. REIT-only portfolios, while offering diversification within real estate, remain exposed to sector-specific cycles and economic factors. Maintaining discipline during periods of market volatility or dividend variability requires an investor mindset attuned to long-term objectives and tolerant of short-term noise. Educational resources, peer discussions, and professional advice can support this psychological resilience, enabling investors to capitalise on compounding and reinvestment opportunities.

Case studies illustrate the diversity of successful REIT portfolio designs. One investor approaching retirement may prioritise high-quality healthcare and residential REITs, complemented by industrial trusts for moderate growth, emphasising income stability and capital preservation. Another, earlier in their career, might tilt toward technology infrastructure and specialty REITs, accepting income fluctuations in exchange for accelerated portfolio growth. Both approaches reflect thoughtful alignment of portfolio construction with personal goals, risk appetite, and market realities.

In sum, setting up a REIT-only portfolio transcends simple asset selection; it is an exercise in tailored strategy, disciplined analysis, and dynamic management. By carefully balancing income and growth, diversifying across sectors and geographies, and maintaining alignment with investor-specific objectives, REIT investors can build portfolios that deliver not only financial returns but also the stability and resilience essential for enduring wealth creation. This foundational understanding equips readers to transition from passive observers of real estate markets to confident, strategic participants shaping their own financial futures.

Avoiding Paralysis by Analysis

For many investors, the promise of Real Estate Investment Trusts (REITs) as a vehicle for income generation and portfolio diversification is tempered by a pervasive hesitation—a reluctance to commit capital amid a swirl of questions about market timing, dividend stability, and valuation integrity. This hesitation often manifests as paralysis by analysis, a condition where the accumulation of information and competing perspectives creates indecision rather than clarity. Understanding and overcoming this paralysis is essential to transforming potential into performance, enabling investors to engage decisively with REITs rather than remain sidelined by uncertainty.

At the heart of paralysis by analysis lies the mistaken belief that one can predict or control market movements with sufficient precision to optimise entry points. Market timing, especially in complex asset classes like REITs, is notoriously elusive. The real estate sector is influenced by multifaceted factors—interest rates, economic cycles, demographic trends, and geopolitical events—that defy simple forecasting. Waiting for the "perfect" moment often results in missed opportunities and diminished compounding benefits. Instead, empirical evidence supports systematic, consistent investment approaches such as dollar-cost averaging, where periodic purchases smooth out price fluctuations and reduce the impact of short-term volatility.

Dividend fluctuations represent another common source of investor anxiety. REITs distribute a substantial portion of earnings as dividends, making income stability a critical consideration. Yet, dividends are not guaranteed; economic downturns, tenant defaults, or capital expenditure demands can precipitate reductions. This variability can alarm investors accustomed to fixed income or traditional bond-like securities. Recognising that dividend volatility is a natural reflection of business cycles rather than a sign of fundamental failure reframes expectations. A well-constructed REIT portfolio, diversified across sectors and geographies, mitigates the impact of individual dividend fluctuations, supporting a more resilient income stream over time.

Valuation anxiety compounds these challenges. Unlike equities whose prices are subject to real-time market discovery, REIT valuations often integrate appraisal-based assessments subject to lag and subjectivity. Investors may struggle to reconcile share price movements with underlying asset values or feel uncertain about the true worth of their holdings. This ambiguity can lead to hesitation, particularly when headlines highlight market corrections or sector downturns. Anchoring valuation analysis in fundamentals—such as funds from operations (FFO), net asset value (NAV), and cash flow stability—offers a more reliable framework. Coupled with an awareness of broader economic indicators and interest rate environments, this approach tempers reactive decision-making.

Mindset tools are invaluable in breaking free from indecision. Cultivating a long-term perspective encourages viewing REIT investments as part of an evolving portfolio journey rather than isolated, time-sensitive bets. Emphasising process over perfection shifts focus to disciplined, repeatable actions—regular contributions, reinvestment of dividends, and periodic portfolio reviews—rather than elusive timing. Cognitive behavioural strategies, including awareness of emotional biases like loss aversion and confirmation bias, empower investors to recognise when anxiety or overanalysis distort judgment.

Practical frameworks also aid in overcoming paralysis. Establishing clear investment objectives aligned with liquidity needs, income requirements, and growth aspirations provides a decision-making anchor. Predefining asset allocation targets and rebalancing rules creates guardrails that reduce ad hoc, emotion-driven choices. Engaging trusted advisors or leveraging digital tools for portfolio monitoring introduces external discipline and real-time feedback, enhancing confidence.

Real-world examples underscore the cost of inaction driven by overanalysis. Investors who delayed initial REIT exposure during market downturns often missed subsequent recoveries and dividend resumption, illustrating opportunity costs. Conversely, those who embraced steady investing despite uncertainty benefited from compounding returns and income accumulation. Such cases affirm that imperfect action informed by rigorous framework consistently outperforms waiting for certainty that seldom arrives.

Ethical reflections arise when considering paralysis by analysis in the context of financial empowerment. Prolonged indecision may reinforce wealth disparities by favouring those with prior assets or professional guidance. Facilitating investor education, transparency, and accessible tools contributes to bridging this gap, enabling broader participation in REIT investing. This perspective highlights that overcoming analytical paralysis is not merely a technical skill but a step toward inclusive financial opportunity.

Navigating the tension between thorough analysis and decisive action demands balance. While rigorous due diligence and ongoing education remain non-negotiable, investors must guard against the paralysis induced by excessive data or conflicting opinions. Developing a personal investment philosophy rooted in clarity, resilience, and adaptability fosters a mindset where analysis informs rather than inhibits. This equilibrium empowers investors to harness the benefits of REITs confidently and consistently.

Ultimately, avoiding paralysis by analysis transforms the investment experience from one of hesitation and missed potential to purposeful engagement and progressive wealth building. By confronting fears around market timing, dividend variability, and valuation uncertainty with disciplined strategies and thoughtful mindset tools, investors unlock the capacity to act decisively. This shift not only advances individual financial goals but also enriches the collective narrative around accessible, informed, and effective real estate investing.

From Transactional to Strategic

The temptation to approach REIT investing as a series of isolated transactions—a quick purchase here, a sale there—is both natural and widespread. After all, modern financial markets offer unprecedented ease of access, instant execution, and real-time pricing that can seduce even seasoned investors into viewing REIT shares as just another commodity to be traded. However, this transactional mindset risks obscuring the profound advantages embedded in adopting REITs as a strategic, long-term investment vehicle. Transforming the approach from short-term speculation to deliberate strategy unlocks compounding power, mitigates behavioral pitfalls, and fosters enduring wealth accumulation rooted in real estate's unique characteristics.

At the core of this strategic reframing lies the concept of reinvestment plans, which encourage investors to systematically channel dividends back into acquiring additional shares rather than extracting income immediately. This practice leverages the "snowball effect" of compounding—dividends generate new units that, in turn, produce their own dividends, setting in motion an exponential growth trajectory. Unlike direct ownership of physical property, where reinvestment often entails large, infrequent capital commitments, REITs enable incremental, disciplined growth with minimal friction. Over time, the cumulative impact of reinvested dividends can rival or exceed capital appreciation, underscoring the importance of patience and consistency.

Complementing reinvestment is the technique of dollar-cost averaging (DCA), which transforms market volatility from a source of anxiety into an opportunity. By investing a fixed amount of capital at regular intervals regardless of price fluctuations, investors purchase more shares when prices are low and fewer when prices are high. This systematic approach avoids the pitfalls of attempting to time entry points—a notoriously unreliable endeavor—and smooths the average cost basis over multiple market cycles. In the context of REITs, where dividend yields can fluctuate and economic cycles impact asset valuations, DCA offers a disciplined method to build exposure without succumbing to emotional reactions or market noise.

The strategic lens also demands reframing expectations about portfolio growth and income generation. REITs, by regulatory design, distribute the majority of taxable income to shareholders, which can produce attractive current yields but may limit internal capital accumulation for growth. A long-term strategy balances these dynamics by combining immediate income needs with the reinvestment imperative, creating a dual engine of value creation. Investors who focus solely on yield without appreciating the power of compounding dividends risk stagnation, while those who pursue growth without regard to income may sacrifice necessary cash flow. Strategic REIT investing synthesises these objectives, tailoring allocations to individual financial goals and time horizons.

Behavioral finance insights further illuminate the benefits of a strategic approach. Frequent trading driven by short-term market reactions tends to amplify losses, increase transaction costs, and induce tax inefficiencies. Conversely, adopting a buy-and-hold philosophy aligned with systematic reinvestment reduces these frictions and guards against cognitive biases such as loss aversion and recency bias. For instance, during periods of market downturn or dividend cuts—common occurrences in real estate cycles—investors anchored in strategy are less likely to capitulate to panic selling, thereby preserving long-term compounding benefits.

Case studies reinforce these principles. Consider an investor who commenced investing in a diversified REIT ETF during a market correction, consistently reinvesting dividends and contributing monthly capital over a decade. Despite interim volatility and sector-specific downturns, the portfolio's compounded growth and income generation eclipsed that of counterparts who traded reactively or withheld capital awaiting "better" entry points. This example illustrates how strategic discipline, more than market timing, drives superior outcomes.

The shift from transactional to strategic also entails embracing technological tools and professional advice that support long-term planning. Digital platforms offering automated dividend reinvestment, portfolio rebalancing alerts, and tax-efficient account integration simplify adherence to strategic frameworks. Engaging financial advisors or leveraging curated model portfolios can further enhance alignment between investment actions and financial objectives, providing structure and accountability that counterbalance emotional impulses.

Ethical reflection complements strategic investment practice. The empowerment derived from adopting a long-term approach fosters financial resilience and autonomy, enabling investors to withstand market vicissitudes without resorting to high-risk gambles or unsustainable behaviours. This discipline also supports broader economic stability by encouraging capital allocation based on fundamental value rather than speculative fervour. Thus, the personal virtue of strategic investing resonates beyond individual portfolios, contributing to healthier market ecosystems.

In sum, repositioning REIT investing from a transactional exercise to a strategic commitment transforms how investors engage with real estate exposure. By harnessing reinvestment, dollar-cost averaging, and the exponential force of compounding within a disciplined framework, investors unlock the full spectrum of benefits REITs offer. This evolution demands mindset shifts, patience, and methodical execution—but the rewards manifest in portfolios that not only grow but endure, reflecting real estate's enduring role as a foundation for lasting wealth.

Chapter 7
REITs Inside Mutual Funds and ETFs

Within the evolving landscape of real estate investment, mutual funds and exchange-traded funds (ETFs) have emerged as pivotal conduits for individual investors seeking exposure to Real Estate Investment Trusts (REITs) without the burdens of direct property ownership. These pooled vehicles promise simplicity—a single transaction granting access to a diversified real estate portfolio. Yet beneath this apparent ease lies a more intricate reality, demanding that investors appreciate what they truly own, how costs accumulate, and how strategic choices shape long-term outcomes. This chapter delves beyond the surface, offering a thorough examination of REIT mutual funds and ETFs, their structural subtleties, and the implications for the discerning investor.

At the most basic level, mutual funds and ETFs operate on contrasting principles. Mutual funds, often actively managed, pool capital to purchase a curated basket of REITs and related assets, with portfolio managers making deliberate selections to achieve targeted outcomes. ETFs, largely passive, track a specified REIT index, replicating its performance with transparency and generally lower costs. These distinctions are far from trivial: mutual funds may promise the potential for outperformance but typically come with higher fees and less intra-day liquidity; ETFs offer continuous pricing and trading flexibility, though they can introduce market-cap biases. Navigating these trade-offs—between cost, control, and exposure—requires thoughtful consideration.

Fees, often underestimated, warrant particular attention. Expense ratios differ widely: actively managed mutual funds frequently exceed 1%, while ETFs may charge under 0.5%. Small as these percentages may seem, over time they compound significantly, eroding net returns. Transaction costs, bid-ask spreads, and tax inefficiencies—especially concerning capital gains distributions and REIT dividend treatment—further affect performance. Such factors underline that investing in pooled REIT vehicles is never cost-neutral; careful assessment aligned with personal circumstances is essential.

Liquidity, another nuanced factor, shapes how investors interact with these funds. ETFs trade like stocks, offering intraday liquidity and price discovery, while mutual funds transact once daily at net asset value. This distinction informs strategy: ETFs facilitate tactical adjustments and opportunistic rebalancing, whereas mutual funds better suit a buy-and-hold philosophy. Yet liquidity can be a double-edged sword; easy access may encourage overtrading, generating higher costs and tax liabilities, potentially undermining long-term outcomes.

Investors must also remain vigilant against exposure overlap. The universe of publicly traded REITs is relatively concentrated, and holding multiple funds can inadvertently amplify sector or issuer-specific risk. For example, a combination of global REIT ETFs may overweight logistics or data centre holdings, distorting intended diversification. Diligent review of fund composition and correlation metrics is crucial to construct genuinely balanced allocations, reducing concentration risk while optimising returns.

The assumption that passive investing—often synonymous with ETFs—is inherently safe is equally misleading. Performance remains tethered to broader real estate market dynamics, interest rates, and economic cycles. Passive funds provide efficient participation in these trends but do not shield investors from sector downturns, dividend pressures, or valuation shifts. Educated, realistic expectations are therefore indispensable.

Choosing between direct REIT ownership and pooled fund structures hinges on factors such as time, expertise, risk tolerance, and conviction. Direct holdings afford granular control, allowing tailored exposure to sectors, geographies, or specific business models, but demand rigorous due diligence, active monitoring, and the ability to manage liquidity and governance challenges. Funds, conversely, offer scalability, diversification, and professional oversight, suiting investors prioritising convenience and broad market exposure. Many sophisticated investors blend both approaches, balancing direct positions with fund allocations to optimise portfolio construction.

Throughout this chapter, real-world examples illuminate these considerations. One investor, for instance, complements a broadly diversified REIT ETF with selective high-conviction individual REITs, blending the simplicity of pooled exposure with targeted control. Other cases highlight how fee differentials and tax implications materially affect net returns, reinforcing the importance of looking beyond headline yield figures.

Ultimately, this discussion challenges the notion that fund investing is passive or hands-off. Instead, it advocates an engaged, informed approach: one in which investors understand structure, cost, liquidity, and strategy, using this knowledge to make deliberate, confident choices. REIT mutual funds and ETFs, when navigated with insight and strategic clarity, become powerful instruments for accessing real estate's potential efficiently and sustainably. Mastery of these vehicles equips investors to discern when to embrace pooled investing and when to exercise direct agency—advancing a sophisticated, adaptable pathway to building wealth in the modern real estate market.

Bundled Simplicity, Layered Complexity

The appeal of Real Estate Investment Trusts (REITs) packaged within mutual funds and exchange-traded funds (ETFs) lies in their promise of bundled simplicity—a single purchase granting access to a diversified real estate portfolio otherwise inaccessible to many investors. This façade of straightforwardness conceals a deeper intricacy. Understanding how REIT funds function, the advantages they confer, and the inherent trade-offs compared to owning individual REIT shares is fundamental for investors who seek not just convenience, but also strategic control and clarity over their real estate exposure.

At their core, mutual funds and ETFs aggregate investor capital to purchase a basket of REITs, each with distinct operational models and risk profiles. Mutual funds are typically actively managed, with portfolio managers selecting securities to outperform benchmarks, relying on research, market insights, and discretionary judgement. ETFs predominantly operate passively, tracking indices composed of publicly traded REITs to mirror market performance with minimal human intervention. This structural distinction shapes investor experience: mutual funds might promise alpha generation through active management but come with higher fees and reduced liquidity, while ETFs offer transparency, tradability, and often lower costs, yet forgo active decision-making.

The simplicity of buying a single fund share masks several layers of complexity. Expense ratios, for example, differ markedly. Actively managed REIT mutual funds can charge fees exceeding 1%, whereas some ETFs trade at fractions of that cost. Over time, these differences compound, eroding total returns. Beyond explicit fees, hidden costs include trading commissions within funds, bid-ask spreads on ETFs, and tax inefficiencies arising from portfolio turnover or capital gains distributions. The net impact on an investor's bottom line can be substantial, making fee vigilance an essential aspect of fund evaluation.

Liquidity nuances further complicate the picture. ETFs provide intraday liquidity, allowing investors to trade throughout market hours with price transparency. Mutual funds transact once daily at net asset value (NAV), offering less immediacy but often smoother pricing. This liquidity influences strategy: ETFs facilitate tactical reallocations and rapid responses to market events, while mutual funds align better with buy-and-hold philosophies. However, higher liquidity does not guarantee better outcomes; it may encourage frequent trading, which increases transaction costs and can undermine compounding.

Diversification within REIT funds is a double-edged sword. While pooling broadens exposure across sectors—such as retail, healthcare, industrial, and residential—it can inadvertently concentrate risk due to overlap among underlying holdings. The publicly traded REIT universe is limited in size and market capitalization, leading multiple funds to hold significant positions in the same top issuers. This redundancy can dilute the benefits of diversification, exposing investors to sector or company-specific shocks despite a superficially broad portfolio. Investors must scrutinise fund holdings to avoid unintended concentration risk and ensure alignment with their risk tolerance.

Comparing fund investing with direct REIT ownership reveals a tension between convenience and control. Individual REIT investments afford the ability to target specific sectors, geographies, or business models and to respond directly to corporate developments or market opportunities. They require diligent research, continuous monitoring, and greater capital commitment to achieve diversification. Conversely, funds offer instant diversification, professional management, and simplified administration but at the cost of less granular control and potential misalignment with individual convictions. This dichotomy underscores that fund investing is not inherently passive; it demands informed oversight to navigate its layered complexity effectively.

Investors must also grapple with the misconception that passive fund investing equates to effortless or risk-free participation. REIT funds remain subject to market volatility, interest rate sensitivity, and economic cycles that affect real estate fundamentals. Performance depends on the underlying assets' quality and sectoral dynamics, irrespective of fund structure. The illusion of simplicity should not obscure the need for strategic engagement, periodic portfolio review, and an understanding of macroeconomic influences on real estate sectors.

Real-world examples illuminate these complexities. Consider the performance divergence between a low-cost REIT ETF tracking a broad index and an actively managed REIT mutual fund with higher fees but concentrated sector bets. The ETF may outperform during stable market conditions due to cost efficiency, while the mutual fund might excel in niche sectors or volatile periods through active repositioning. Another scenario involves investors inadvertently holding multiple REIT funds with overlapping holdings, resulting in concentrated exposure to retail REITs during a sector downturn. These cases highlight the necessity of discerning fund selection tailored to investment goals and risk profiles.

Philosophically, the juxtaposition of bundled simplicity with layered complexity invites reflection on the nature of investment choices in contemporary markets. While funds democratise access and lower barriers, they also require investors to cultivate sophistication to decode structures, costs, and risks embedded beneath the surface.

This dynamic challenges the notion that ease of access justifies passive acceptance; rather, it demands active learning and strategic decision-making to harness real estate investing's full potential.

In synthesising these insights, investors emerge better equipped to evaluate when pooled REIT investments serve as efficient vehicles and when direct ownership aligns more closely with personal objectives. Recognising the multi-dimensional nature of REIT mutual funds and ETFs transforms them from black-box solutions into tools of nuanced portfolio construction. By embracing this duality—valuing convenience while respecting complexity—investors can navigate the real estate landscape with clarity and confidence, ultimately shaping portfolios that reflect both pragmatic accessibility and strategic depth.

Fees, Liquidity, and Overlap

When considering investments in REIT mutual funds and ETFs, three interconnected factors—fees, liquidity, and portfolio overlap—demand rigorous scrutiny. Each influences the net returns, risk profile, and operational ease of owning these vehicles, shaping the investor's experience and ultimate financial outcomes. Understanding how to assess these elements is crucial, as they often operate beneath the surface of headline yields and fund names, quietly eroding gains or amplifying vulnerabilities if left unchecked.

The most immediate and tangible cost is the expense ratio, a measure of the annual fees charged by fund managers to cover administrative, management, and operational expenses. While often presented as a simple percentage, the compounding effect of expense ratios over time can significantly reduce total returns. For instance, an expense ratio of 1% may seem modest, but over two decades, it can diminish compounded growth by nearly a third compared to a zero-fee investment. This impact is particularly pronounced in REIT funds, where dividend yields might be attractive but net income is sensitive to fee drag. Investors must therefore prioritise low-cost funds without sacrificing quality or strategic alignment. ETFs, with their passive management style, generally offer lower expense ratios than actively managed mutual funds, but this is not universally true, especially in niche or international REIT segments.

Beyond headline fees, investors encounter additional, less obvious costs. Bid-ask spreads—the difference between the price buyers are willing to pay and sellers are asking—can widen considerably in thinly traded ETFs or niche REIT mutual funds, increasing transaction costs. Furthermore, trading commissions, though often minimal today, can accumulate with frequent buying and selling, eroding returns especially for smaller investors. Tax implications also intertwine with costs: REIT dividends, largely classified as ordinary income rather than qualified dividends, are taxed at higher rates for many investors. Mutual funds may distribute capital gains that trigger unexpected tax bills, particularly if the fund manager engages in frequent portfolio turnover. Awareness of these layered expenses enables investors to gauge the true cost of fund ownership and to deploy tax-efficient strategies, such as investing within tax-advantaged accounts or choosing funds with low turnover.

Liquidity—the ease with which an investment can be bought or sold without materially affecting its price—is another critical consideration. ETFs, traded on exchanges throughout the day, offer near-instant liquidity and transparent pricing, empowering investors to react swiftly to market conditions or rebalance portfolios. Mutual funds, by contrast, execute trades only once per day after market close, at net asset value. While this might limit tactical flexibility, it also can reduce impulsive trading driven by short-term volatility. However, not all ETFs are equally liquid; funds tracking obscure REIT sectors or smaller markets may experience low trading volumes, leading to larger bid-ask spreads and price inefficiencies. Investors must balance the desire for liquidity with their investment horizon and the potential cost of trading.

Closely related to fees and liquidity is the issue of portfolio overlap and concentration risk. The universe of publicly traded REITs, while broadening, remains relatively limited in scale and dominated by a handful of large-cap entities. As a result, multiple REIT mutual funds and ETFs often hold significant stakes in the same core companies, particularly those in dominant sectors such as retail, industrial logistics, or data centres. This overlap can create an illusion of diversification while exposing investors to sector-specific or issuer-specific shocks. For example, an investor unknowingly holding several funds might find their portfolio disproportionately weighted toward a struggling retail REIT during economic downturns, exacerbating losses. Evaluating overlap requires reviewing fund holdings and sector allocations carefully, a process complicated by varying disclosure standards and frequent portfolio changes. Tools such as portfolio correlation matrices or third-party analysis platforms can assist in quantifying overlap and guiding rebalancing decisions.

Addressing these challenges involves trade-offs and informed prioritisation. Lower-fee funds may exclude niche or specialty REITs, potentially limiting growth opportunities or income stability. High liquidity may tempt investors into short-term trading, undermining compounding benefits. Efforts to reduce overlap might sacrifice simplicity or increase transaction complexity. Consequently, investors should define clear investment objectives—whether income generation, growth, or capital preservation—and tailor fund selection accordingly, recognising that no single fund perfectly satisfies all criteria.

Real-world case studies exemplify these dynamics. An investor who selects a low-cost broad-market REIT ETF may benefit from cost efficiency and liquidity but encounter unexpected overlap if supplementing with sector-specific funds. Another investor prioritising income might favour actively managed mutual funds with higher fees, justifying the cost through potential yield enhancement and risk mitigation. However, without vigilant monitoring of fees and tax consequences, even well-intentioned strategies can erode net returns. Such examples reinforce the need for a holistic approach that integrates fee awareness, liquidity considerations, and portfolio construction to optimise REIT fund investments.

Ethically, the investor's responsibility extends beyond personal gain to include awareness of how fee structures and fund management practices impact broader market integrity and fairness. Excessive fees can privilege institutional managers at the expense of individual investors, while opaque liquidity and overlap issues may propagate systemic risks through correlated exposures. Advocating for transparency, competitive pricing, and investor education contributes to a healthier investment ecosystem.

In mastering the interplay of fees, liquidity, and overlap, investors not only enhance their capacity to navigate REIT funds judiciously but also cultivate a mindset attuned to the nuanced realities of real estate investing. This vigilance transforms seemingly straightforward investment choices into strategic decisions grounded in clarity and foresight, ultimately fostering portfolios that reflect both sophistication and resilience.

Passive Doesn't Mean Passive Returns

The term "passive investing" carries an almost mythical allure, often conjuring images of effortless wealth accumulation through low-cost, hands-off exposure to broad market indices. Exchange-traded funds (ETFs), particularly those tracking REIT indices, are frequently positioned within this narrative as an accessible, "safe" pathway into real estate investing. Yet, beneath this appealing veneer lies a more nuanced reality: passive investing is neither effortless nor inherently low risk. The ultimate performance of any REIT ETF is inexorably tied to the underlying assets' market dynamics, economic cycles, and sector-specific vulnerabilities. Recognising this distinction is vital for investors to approach REIT funds with both eyes open and expectations properly calibrated.

At the heart of this misconception is a conflation between the operational simplicity of ETF investing and the complexity of the markets they represent. Passive funds aim to replicate the performance of a specified index, minimizing active management and transaction costs. This structure can reduce fee drag and mitigate manager risk, yet it does not immunise investors from market volatility or sector downturns. For example, during periods of rising interest rates—a historically significant headwind for REITs—passive REIT ETFs can suffer substantial price declines alongside their underlying holdings. This volatility directly challenges the notion that "set and forget" investing automatically equates to safety or predictability.

Moreover, the label "passive" obscures the crucial decision-making that investors must still engage in, such as selecting appropriate funds, determining asset allocation, and managing risk exposures. The breadth of REIT ETFs varies widely: some track broad-based indices encompassing diverse sectors and geographies, while others specialise in niche areas like healthcare facilities or data centres. Each carries distinct risk-return profiles influenced by economic fundamentals, regulatory environments, and demographic trends. Investors who overlook these nuances risk unintended concentration or exposure to sectors experiencing structural challenges, undermining the benefits of diversification.

Real-world episodes highlight the consequences of passive investing misconceptions. The 2020 COVID-19 pandemic, for instance, devastated certain REIT sectors like retail malls and hospitality, while boosting demand for logistics and data centre properties. A passive investor in a broad REIT ETF bore the brunt of sector-specific losses, despite the fund's low fees and diversified mandate. Conversely, more active or sector-focused investors could reposition portfolios to capitalise on emerging trends, underscoring that passive investing does not guarantee superior risk management or alpha preservation.

Underlying all these considerations is the reality that REIT returns depend fundamentally on property-level performance—rental income, occupancy rates, lease structures, and capital expenditures—none of which are controlled or altered by a passive fund's replication strategy. Consequently, external economic shocks, regulatory changes, and shifts in consumer behaviour can directly influence dividend sustainability and capital appreciation, impacting ETF prices. Investors must therefore maintain vigilance over macroeconomic indicators and sector health, even when holding passively managed funds.

The tax treatment of REIT distributions further complicates the passive investing narrative. REIT dividends are generally classified as ordinary income rather than qualified dividends, attracting higher tax rates for many investors. Passive fund structures can generate capital gains distributions through portfolio turnover, adding unexpected tax liabilities. Without active tax planning or utilisation of tax-advantaged accounts, passive investors may face a heavier tax burden than anticipated, eroding after-tax returns.

Ethically, the promotion of passive investing as a near-automatic path to financial security risks fostering complacency and unrealistic expectations among retail investors. While lowering barriers to market participation is commendable, transparent education about inherent risks and performance drivers is essential to empower informed decision-making. Investors who appreciate that passive investing demands ongoing attention and strategic context are better positioned to navigate market complexities with discipline and resilience.

Ultimately, the phrase "passive investing" describes an investment management style, not an investment outcome. The returns generated by REIT ETFs remain subject to the cyclical nature of real estate markets, interest rate fluctuations, and broader economic forces. Investors who embrace this reality, integrating passive vehicles within a well-considered, actively monitored portfolio framework, can harness the cost efficiencies of indexing without surrendering strategic agency. This balanced approach transforms passive REIT investing from a misleadingly simple concept into a sophisticated component of long-term wealth building.

When to Go Direct, When to Stay Pooled

Investing in real estate investment trusts (REITs) presents investors with a fundamental strategic choice: to purchase shares of individual REITs directly or to invest through pooled vehicles such as mutual funds and exchange-traded funds (ETFs). This decision is neither trivial nor universal; it depends on a nuanced interplay of factors including the investor's available time, level of expertise, risk tolerance, and conviction in specific sectors or companies. The clarity of this choice is essential, as each approach offers distinct advantages and pitfalls that can materially affect portfolio outcomes. To navigate this landscape effectively requires a deliberate framework rooted in practical realities and informed judgment.

Direct ownership of individual REITs appeals primarily to investors who seek granular control and targeted exposure. By selecting specific REITs, investors can tailor their portfolios to particular sectors—such as healthcare, industrial logistics, or data centres—aligning with their market outlook or thematic convictions. This approach demands a considerable investment of time and analytical effort to evaluate company fundamentals, assess management quality, and monitor operational performance. Seasoned investors with expertise in real estate markets may derive superior returns by identifying undervalued or mispriced REITs, capitalising on sector trends, or avoiding structural weaknesses. However, direct investment inherently increases concentration risk; poor performance in a single REIT can disproportionately impact overall portfolio results.

Conversely, pooled investments offer diversification and convenience. Mutual funds and ETFs that track broad or sector-specific REIT indices provide instant exposure to a wide array of properties and management teams, mitigating the idiosyncratic risks of individual holdings. This diversification can smooth returns and reduce volatility, appealing to investors who lack the time or inclination for detailed company research. Pooled funds often come with professional management and lower transaction costs relative to building a comparable portfolio of individual REITs. However, investors cede control over holdings and may encounter unintended overlap with other portfolio components. Moreover, fees—while often modest—can erode returns, particularly in actively managed funds.

Investor time horizon and liquidity needs further influence the direct versus pooled choice. For long-term investors prioritising steady income and capital preservation, diversified REIT ETFs offer a low-maintenance vehicle that aligns with buy-and-hold strategies. Those with shorter time horizons or tactical investment goals might prefer individual REITs to exploit market dislocations or sector rotations, accepting greater monitoring demands and volatility. Similarly, investors requiring immediate liquidity may find ETFs more suitable due to their intraday tradability, whereas mutual funds impose daily pricing and redemption constraints, and direct holdings vary in liquidity depending on market capitalisation and trading volumes.

Conviction level and confidence in analytical capabilities constitute another critical axis. Investors equipped with deep sector knowledge, access to proprietary research, or a strong understanding of real estate fundamentals are better positioned to identify direct investment opportunities with potential for outperformance. Conversely, novice or passive investors benefit from the risk mitigation and professional oversight embedded in pooled funds. This dynamic reflects a broader investment principle: higher potential reward through direct exposure accompanies increased responsibility and risk.

Technological advancements and platforms have lowered barriers to direct REIT ownership, enabling fractional shares and reduced minimum investment thresholds. While this democratises access, it also exposes investors to pitfalls if decision-making is not grounded in rigorous analysis. The abundance of available data and fund offerings can overwhelm, prompting suboptimal choices or herd behaviour. In contrast, pooled funds distil complexity into a manageable product, but the "black box" nature of fund management can obscure risks or dilute returns.

A notable tension arises between cost efficiency and bespoke strategy. Direct investments eliminate fund management fees but may incur higher transaction costs and demand ongoing research. Pooled funds benefit from economies of scale and simplified execution but impose management fees that accumulate over time. Quantifying this trade-off involves considering investment size, trading frequency, and expected outperformance from active selection.

Ethical considerations intersect with these strategic decisions. Transparency and alignment of interests become paramount when entrusting capital to fund managers. Investors must critically evaluate whether fee structures, incentive models, and governance practices promote long-term value creation or merely extract rents. Direct investors bear the onus of due diligence, whereas pooled investors delegate stewardship, underscoring the importance of choosing reputable funds and managers.

Illustrative case studies illuminate these dynamics. An investor focused on retirement income might construct a diversified REIT ETF portfolio to balance yield and risk, utilising dollar-cost averaging and automatic dividend reinvestment. Conversely, a real estate professional with specialised expertise may concentrate holdings in niche industrial REITs poised to benefit from e-commerce growth, accepting heightened volatility in pursuit of alpha. Both approaches can succeed when aligned with investor profile and discipline.

Ultimately, the decision to go direct or remain pooled hinges on a matrix of personal attributes and market realities. The most prudent investors integrate both pathways, employing pooled funds as a foundational core while selectively adding individual REITs to express informed convictions. This hybrid strategy combines diversification with tactical precision, leveraging the strengths of each modality without overcommitting to their respective weaknesses.

Mastering this balance transforms REIT investing from a binary choice into a dynamic, evolving strategy responsive to changing objectives, market conditions, and individual growth as an investor. With clear frameworks and disciplined execution, one can navigate the direct versus pooled dilemma confidently, harnessing the full potential of REITs as a cornerstone of a modern investment portfolio.

Chapter 8
Going Global—REITs Beyond Borders

The appeal of international real estate investment is immediate and visceral. Many investors instinctively see geographic diversification as a shield—a way to hedge against local downturns while accessing growth opportunities in unfamiliar markets. Yet beneath this straightforward narrative lies a far more intricate landscape. Geographic spread alone does not automatically reduce risk. Economic cycles, currency swings, legal frameworks, and cultural nuances all interact to shape the performance and volatility of global real estate investment trusts (REITs). To build a resilient, profitable international portfolio, an investor must grapple with these interwoven forces rather than rely on geography as a simple safety net.

The notion that merely allocating capital across multiple countries ensures diversification overlooks the deep interconnections of global markets. Recessions, crises, and financial shocks rarely respect borders; downturns in one region can cascade elsewhere. Currency fluctuations, too, can silently erode returns, often undermining the benefits of passive diversification. Beyond these macroeconomic factors, each nation imposes its own regulatory and tax regime, which influences REIT governance, income distribution, and growth prospects. Recognising these nuances is critical; a superficial approach to international diversification can generate the illusion of safety while masking underlying risks.

Case studies across Asia, Europe, and emerging markets illustrate the complexity—and opportunity—of global REIT investment. Japan's REIT market, for instance, is heavily weighted toward logistics assets, reflecting the rise of e-commerce and supply chain optimisation. Singapore's healthcare REITs, by contrast, benefit from stable demographics and a rigorous regulatory framework, offering steady income streams and measured growth. Emerging markets tantalise with the prospect of high returns, yet carry heightened political and regulatory risks. The challenge for investors lies in capturing these sector-specific opportunities while managing the uncertainties that accompany them.

Dividend culture also varies considerably across regions. In many Asian markets, high payout ratios are mandated or customary, making REITs a cornerstone of income-oriented strategies. European REITs often strike a more balanced approach, combining income with capital appreciation in line with local investor preferences and tax regimes. Such differences demand recalibrated expectations: an investor accustomed to U.S. dividend norms may need to rethink assumptions about yield stability and payout consistency when venturing abroad.

Constructing a borderless REIT portfolio is as much an art as a science. Investment channels are diverse, ranging from U.S.-listed international REIT ETFs and mutual funds to direct acquisitions through foreign exchanges or international brokerage platforms. Each route presents trade-offs in liquidity, transparency, fees, and regulatory oversight. Successful global investing requires aligning these practical considerations with individual objectives, risk tolerance, and operational bandwidth. This chapter provides both the conceptual frameworks and actionable guidance needed to navigate this terrain with confidence, enabling portfolio construction that is truly international yet disciplined.

By peeling back misconceptions and illuminating the multifaceted realities of cross-border REIT investment, this discussion offers a strategic lens through which to view the global market. International diversification is not simply about spreading capital geographically; it demands a holistic reconsideration of portfolio theory, risk management, and opportunity recognition. When approached thoughtfully, global REIT investing allows for the full harnessing of real estate's potential as an asset class—delivering income, resilience, and growth to the investor willing to engage with the complexity and nuance of twenty-first-century markets.

Why Geography Is Not Diversification

The common refrain among investors is that international diversification—spreading capital across different countries and regions—is a straightforward recipe for risk reduction. Yet, beneath this seemingly intuitive strategy lies a more intricate truth: geography alone is an insufficient safeguard against volatility and systemic risk.

Especially in the context of Real Estate Investment Trusts (REITs), which themselves operate within complex frameworks influenced by economic cycles, currency dynamics, and regulatory environments, the assumption that simply owning assets across borders equates to diversification warrants rigorous re-examination.

Economic cycles are often synchronised across advanced and emerging markets in ways that undermine naive geographic diversification strategies. The global financial crisis of 2008 serves as a salient example. REITs from disparate regions—North America, Europe, and parts of Asia—experienced simultaneous downturns, as capital markets contracted and credit availability evaporated. This synchronicity challenges the simplistic notion that geographic dispersion necessarily smooths portfolio returns. In fact, contagion effects in an increasingly interconnected world can cause correlation spikes precisely when diversification is most needed. Investors must therefore consider not only geographic spread but the underlying economic linkages that bind markets together.

Currency risk introduces a further layer of complexity. While diversification into foreign markets can mitigate exposure to any single domestic economic downturn, fluctuating exchange rates can significantly amplify or erode returns. For example, an investor holding European REITs denominated in euros may see gains wiped out by a weakening euro relative to their home currency. Conversely, currency appreciation can boost returns, but this volatility introduces an additional dimension of uncertainty not present in domestic holdings. Effective currency risk management is rarely as straightforward as picking diverse geographies; it requires a nuanced understanding of forex markets, central bank policies, and global capital flows.

Regulatory and legal frameworks impose another critical, yet often overlooked, constraint on the benefits of geographic diversification. REIT structures vary widely across jurisdictions, affecting taxation, payout requirements, and operational flexibility. In some countries, REITs are mandated to distribute the majority of taxable income, ensuring steady dividends but limiting reinvestment capacity. Elsewhere, more flexible regimes may allow REITs to retain earnings for growth but with greater volatility in distributions. Such differences influence not only income stability but also the risk-return profile of investments. An investor unfamiliar with these jurisdictional nuances may misjudge the reliability of foreign REIT dividends or the potential for capital appreciation.

Moreover, cultural attitudes toward income and investment horizons shape market behaviour in ways that challenge simplistic diversification assumptions. For instance, some Asian markets exhibit a preference for high dividend yields and conservative payout policies, while certain European REIT markets strike a balance between income and growth, reflecting investor expectations and local market maturity. These cultural factors influence managerial decisions and, by extension, the performance and risk characteristics of REITs. Recognising such distinctions enables investors to align portfolio construction with their income needs and risk tolerance rather than relying solely on geographic dispersion.

To navigate these complexities, investors must adopt a framework that transcends geography and incorporates macroeconomic conditions, currency exposure, legal structures, and cultural investment paradigms. This requires a move away from broad-brush diversification towards a more granular, sector-informed, and risk-managed approach to global REIT investing. For example, an investor might combine logistics-focused REITs in Asia—driven by e-commerce growth—with healthcare REITs in Europe, providing countercyclical income streams amid differing demographic trends. Coupled with currency hedging strategies and careful legal due diligence, such an approach offers more robust diversification than geography alone could deliver.

In practical terms, this means engaging with detailed data on REIT performance across markets, understanding local economic cycles, and critically assessing the interplay between currency movements and dividend policies. It also involves a recognition that the global real estate market is not a monolith but a mosaic of distinct sub-markets, each with its own risk-return characteristics shaped by local forces. Investors who integrate these considerations into their global REIT strategy are better equipped to build portfolios that balance growth and income, reduce systemic vulnerabilities, and capitalise on genuine diversification benefits.

In sum, geography should not be conflated with diversification. The promise of international REIT investing lies not merely in owning assets across borders, but in mastering the intricacies that govern each market's unique environment. Economic interconnectedness, currency fluctuations, regulatory disparities, and cultural factors converge to shape outcomes in ways that challenge naive assumptions. A sophisticated investor approaches global REIT portfolios with eyes wide open—engaging deeply with these variables to construct a truly diversified, resilient investment vehicle. This critical mindset elevates international real estate investing from a geographical scattergun to a strategically calibrated endeavour, aligned with the enduring pursuit of wealth preservation and growth.

REITs in Asia, Europe, and Emerging Markets

The landscape of international REIT markets is a complex tapestry woven from diverse regulatory frameworks, economic trajectories, and sectoral opportunities that vary dramatically across Asia, Europe, and emerging economies. For the discerning investor, understanding these nuances is essential to harnessing the true potential of global real estate investing, rather than relying on broad assumptions or incomplete regional snapshots. As real estate markets evolve in response to demographic shifts, technological innovation, and shifting geopolitical dynamics, the contours of REIT investing reflect both opportunity and challenge in equal measure.

Asia, with its dynamic economies and rapidly urbanising populations, represents a particularly fertile ground for REIT growth, albeit within a fragmented regulatory environment. Japan's logistics sector exemplifies this trend, driven by the country's position as a global manufacturing hub and the exponential rise of e-commerce. Japanese logistics REITs benefit from long-term leases to stable tenants, low vacancy rates, and government incentives aimed at enhancing supply chain resilience. Yet, investors must navigate regulatory peculiarities such as strict zoning laws and a relatively conservative approach to leverage. Singapore, by contrast, has emerged as a beacon of regulatory sophistication and transparency in Asia's REIT space, notably within healthcare real estate. Singapore's healthcare REITs capitalise on an ageing population and robust government healthcare spending, offering investors access to well-managed portfolios of hospitals, nursing homes, and medical office buildings. The city-state's regulatory regime mandates high disclosure standards and dividend payout ratios, underpinning income reliability.

Moving westward, Europe's REIT markets present a mosaic of maturity levels and regulatory architectures. Countries like the United Kingdom and the Netherlands have established frameworks supporting well-capitalised REITs that span office, retail, and residential sectors. The UK's REIT regime, introduced in 2007, has fostered a diversified REIT ecosystem that includes specialist sectors such as student accommodation and data centres. However, the continent's heterogeneous legal systems and tax regimes require investors to exercise granular due diligence. For instance, while some European REITs offer compelling dividend yields, others operate under constraints that limit payout flexibility or expose investors to higher withholding taxes. Additionally, the European market has witnessed increasing interest in sustainability-focused REITs, aligned with the European Union's Green Deal and growing investor demand for environmental, social, and governance (ESG) compliance.

Emerging markets present a more uneven yet tantalising prospect. Countries such as India, Brazil, and parts of Southeast Asia are at various stages of developing their REIT ecosystems, often hampered by regulatory ambiguity and nascent capital markets. India's Real Estate Investment Trusts, for example, were only formally recognised in 2014 but have since attracted attention due to rapid urbanisation and government reforms promoting affordable housing and infrastructure development. Despite high growth potential, investors face challenges including limited liquidity, valuation opacity, and higher perceived risks linked to political and economic volatility. Brazil's real estate market, buoyed by commodities wealth and expanding middle-class consumption, offers niche REIT plays in logistics and commercial real estate, yet currency fluctuations and inflationary pressures remain formidable headwinds.

A recurring theme across these geographies is the imperative to understand sector-specific dynamics alongside regulatory and macroeconomic factors. Logistics properties in Japan benefit from technological integration and supply chain optimisation; healthcare real estate in Singapore thrives on demographic trends and policy support; European data centres leverage the continent's digital transformation; emerging market retail REITs navigate shifting consumer patterns and infrastructure gaps. Such specificity enables investors to move beyond broad-brush geographic allocations towards portfolios that integrate thematic insights with regional expertise.

Moreover, global REIT investors must grapple with operational and strategic differences in management approaches. Asian and emerging market REIT managers often exhibit a blend of entrepreneurial agility and adaptation to rapidly changing local market conditions, contrasting with the more institutionalised governance and risk management frameworks prevalent in Europe. This divergence affects not only performance stability but also transparency and corporate governance standards, critical factors for risk-conscious investors.

The increasing globalization of capital markets has also facilitated access to these diverse REIT opportunities through cross-listed vehicles and international ETFs, allowing investors to tailor exposure without direct engagement in foreign exchanges. Yet, this convenience demands sophisticated understanding of cross-border tax implications, currency hedging strategies, and the trade-offs inherent in pooled versus direct ownership structures.

In sum, the international REIT landscape defies simplistic categorisation. Asia's robust growth sectors and regulatory strides, Europe's blend of mature and evolving markets, and the high-risk, high-reward environment of emerging economies collectively expand the real estate investor's toolkit. Success in this domain requires not only a keen eye for macroeconomic and sectoral trends but a disciplined approach to regulatory and operational nuances. Those who master these complexities position themselves to capture the diverse opportunities of a truly global REIT portfolio—where geographic reach meets strategic precision, and where the promise of real estate wealth extends far beyond domestic borders.

The Global Dividend Culture

Dividend reliability is often the cornerstone upon which income investors build their real estate investment strategies. Yet, the stability and predictability of dividends vary widely across global REIT markets, shaped not only by economic fundamentals but by deeply ingrained cultural attitudes towards income, risk, and corporate governance. Understanding these variations is essential for investors seeking to navigate the global REIT landscape with clarity and discernment. The global dividend culture is far from monolithic; rather, it reflects a rich interplay of legal frameworks, investor expectations, and national priorities that collectively influence how REITs distribute income and engage with shareholders.

One of the most striking contrasts emerges when comparing North American and Asian REIT markets. In the United States, REITs are legally required to distribute at least 90% of their taxable income as dividends, fostering a culture of regular, often quarterly payouts. This mandate has entrenched dividend reliability as a defining feature of American REITs, aligning closely with investor demand for predictable income streams, especially among retirees and income-focused portfolios. The regulatory environment, combined with a mature capital market infrastructure, encourages transparency and rigorous disclosure, allowing investors to assess dividend sustainability with relative confidence. This environment nurtures a mindset that equates dividends with financial discipline and operational efficiency, reinforcing the notion that steady payouts signal corporate health.

Contrast this with Japan's REIT market, where cultural attitudes toward income generation and corporate conservatism shape a markedly different dividend profile. Japanese investors tend to favour capital preservation and cautious growth, reflecting broader societal values of stability and long-term security. Consequently, Japanese REITs often adopt more conservative payout policies, balancing dividends with retained earnings to maintain strong balance sheets and fund incremental property acquisitions or upgrades. While dividends are still a critical component, they are typically supplemented by capital appreciation strategies, and payouts may be less predictable than in the US context. This divergence illustrates how local investor psychology can modulate corporate behaviour, even within the same asset class.

Europe offers a heterogeneous picture, shaped by a patchwork of regulatory regimes and cultural norms. Countries like the United Kingdom and the Netherlands exhibit dividend practices akin to those in North America, emphasising steady income distributions bolstered by comprehensive disclosure requirements. Yet other European nations, such as Germany and France, often experience a more nuanced approach, where dividend policies are intertwined with tax considerations and shareholder preferences. For instance, French REITs (SIICs) benefit from favourable tax treatments conditional on high dividend payouts, but market volatility and economic uncertainty sometimes prompt more flexible approaches to income distribution. Investors must therefore evaluate dividend reliability not only through corporate disclosures but also within the context of country-specific tax laws and market conventions.

Emerging markets add further complexity to the global dividend mosaic. In regions such as Latin America and Southeast Asia, REIT markets are nascent or evolving, with regulatory frameworks still maturing. Dividend reliability in these markets can be erratic, reflecting both operational challenges and evolving investor expectations. For example, Singapore's REIT market, while mature and highly regulated, exhibits a dividend culture deeply influenced by its status as a financial hub and its investor base's preference for stable, regular income. Singaporean REITs often feature mandated high payout ratios and stringent governance standards, aligning with a dividend culture that prioritises income over aggressive growth. This contrasts with certain Southeast Asian markets where REITs may offer less predictable income streams, constrained by market liquidity and regulatory uncertainties.

Currency risk and macroeconomic volatility further complicate dividend reliability across borders. Investors holding foreign REITs must contend with exchange rate fluctuations that can erode dividend value even when distributions remain stable in local currency terms. Moreover, economic cycles and policy shifts can lead to dividend cuts or suspensions, particularly in markets where REITs are heavily concentrated in economically sensitive sectors like retail or hospitality. Such risks underscore the importance of a nuanced, multifactor approach to assessing dividend reliability—one that transcends headline yield figures to incorporate macroeconomic, sectoral, and geopolitical analyses.

Crucially, cultural attitudes towards dividend income extend beyond mere payout ratios to encompass broader investor-company dynamics. In markets where dividend income is a primary source of investor return, management teams may face pressure to maintain or increase payouts, potentially at the expense of long-term strategic investments. Conversely, in cultures more accepting of retained earnings for growth, REIT managers may enjoy greater flexibility but must compensate investors through capital appreciation and transparent communication. This tension between immediate income and long-term value creation presents a critical lens through which to evaluate REIT dividend policies globally.

In navigating this global dividend landscape, investors benefit from recognising that dividend reliability is as much a product of cultural context as it is of financial metrics. A REIT's dividend policy cannot be fully understood in isolation from the economic, legal, and social fabric of its home market. Appreciating these subtleties enables investors to calibrate expectations, manage risk, and construct portfolios that reflect not only geographic diversification but also diversification of dividend cultures and income philosophies.

Ultimately, mastering the global dividend culture demands intellectual rigor and cultural sensitivity. It challenges investors to look beyond uniform benchmarks and engage with the rich diversity of income generation strategies worldwide. Those who do so position themselves to capture stable, meaningful income streams while respecting the unique market dynamics that underpin dividend reliability in international REIT investing.

Building a Borderless Portfolio

Accessing global real estate investment trusts (REITs) presents an unparalleled opportunity for investors to diversify beyond domestic borders, tapping into varied economic cycles, regulatory frameworks, and sectoral strengths. Yet, the process of constructing a truly borderless REIT portfolio is nuanced, requiring careful navigation of structural, regulatory, and practical considerations. Whether through U.S.-based vehicles or international brokerage platforms, the pathways to global REIT ownership each carry distinctive benefits and constraints, which demand a rigorous, informed approach to optimise outcomes and mitigate risks.

U.S.-based REIT vehicles, including mutual funds and exchange-traded funds (ETFs), offer an expedient and accessible gateway to international property markets. These pooled investment structures consolidate exposure across multiple global REITs, delivering immediate diversification and professional management without the complexity of direct foreign investment. Investors benefit from simplified account management, transparent fee structures, and the robust regulatory protections afforded by U.S. securities laws. For example, funds like the Vanguard Global ex-U.S. Real Estate ETF or the iShares Global REIT ETF assemble a curated selection of international real estate companies, spanning Asia, Europe, and emerging markets. This approach enables participation in diverse geographies and sectors while minimising administrative burdens, foreign tax reporting, and currency transaction costs typically associated with direct holdings.

However, the convenience of U.S.-based global REIT funds comes with trade-offs that investors must weigh carefully. Fund-level expenses, including management fees and operating costs, erode net returns over time, particularly for those seeking long-term income growth. Furthermore, fund portfolios may suffer from overlapping holdings, inadvertently concentrating risk despite appearing diversified on paper. For instance, many global REIT ETFs heavily weight large-cap REITs domiciled in developed markets, potentially underexposing investors to niche, high-growth sectors in emerging economies. Additionally, while these funds distribute dividends, foreign withholding taxes can reduce yield, and U.S. investors may need to navigate foreign tax credit mechanisms to optimise tax efficiency. Thus, while U.S.-based vehicles democratise access to international real estate, discerning investors must interrogate fund composition, fees, and tax implications to ensure alignment with portfolio objectives.

Direct investment in foreign REITs through international brokers represents an alternative, offering granular control and the potential to exploit market inefficiencies or sector-specific opportunities unavailable in pooled funds. Platforms such as Interactive Brokers or Charles Schwab's Global Account allow investors to purchase shares listed on exchanges across Asia, Europe, and emerging markets. This direct approach enables strategic concentration, enabling investors to tailor exposures to themes like Japan's logistics real estate surge, Singapore's burgeoning healthcare REITs, or the rapid urbanisation driving Latin American property sectors. Moreover, direct ownership can enhance dividend capture by reducing intermediary costs and providing greater visibility into payout schedules and corporate governance.

Yet, this pathway is not without significant complexity and risk. Foreign exchange fluctuations introduce a layer of volatility that can amplify or erode returns independently of underlying asset performance. Settlement procedures, trading hours, and market liquidity vary widely, with some emerging market REITs exhibiting limited daily volume, thereby increasing bid-ask spreads and execution risk. Regulatory disparities create additional hurdles, with varying disclosure standards, accounting practices, and shareholder protections demanding heightened due diligence. Tax treatment of dividends and capital gains differs across jurisdictions, complicating tax reporting and compliance. For example, a U.S. investor holding a European REIT may encounter withholding tax rates exceeding 15%, alongside intricate foreign tax credit claims. Collectively, these factors underscore the necessity of institutional-grade research capabilities or advisory relationships to navigate direct foreign REIT ownership effectively.

Currency risk, a perennial challenge in cross-border investing, warrants particular attention in global REIT portfolios. Currency depreciation in a REIT's home market relative to the investor's base currency can materially diminish income and capital returns. While hedging instruments exist, their cost and complexity may outweigh benefits for retail investors. Strategic asset allocation can mitigate currency exposure through geographic diversification and selective currency-hedged funds. For instance, some global REIT ETFs offer hedged share classes designed to neutralise currency fluctuations, appealing to investors prioritising income stability over capital appreciation.

Legal and regulatory frameworks profoundly influence the feasibility and attractiveness of foreign REIT investments. Countries with mature REIT regimes, such as Singapore, Australia, and parts of Europe, provide clearer governance, tax transparency, and investor rights, enhancing confidence and price discovery. Conversely, markets with evolving REIT laws may present growth opportunities but at elevated legal and operational risk. Investors must assess regulatory stability alongside economic fundamentals, recognising that abrupt policy shifts—such as changes in foreign ownership restrictions or tax regimes—can impair asset values and income streams.

Integrating global REITs into a portfolio also demands a strategic view of correlation dynamics and sectoral complementarity. While geographic diversification aims to reduce portfolio volatility, global real estate markets are increasingly interconnected through capital flows and macroeconomic linkages. Sector-specific risks, such as e-commerce's impact on retail properties or the rise of data centres, may manifest simultaneously across countries, challenging the notion that international diversification alone guarantees risk reduction. Thus, portfolio construction must transcend simplistic geographic allocations, instead employing nuanced analyses of economic cycles, sectoral trends, and regulatory environments.

Technological advances have further lowered barriers to global REIT investing. Online brokerage platforms, digital custodians, and real-time market data access empower individual investors with tools once reserved for institutional players. Robo-advisors and managed portfolio services increasingly incorporate international REIT exposure, facilitating automated diversification aligned with risk profiles and investment horizons. Yet, these innovations do not substitute for investor education and active engagement. Understanding the complexities of foreign market mechanics, tax treaties, and currency risk remains critical to making informed investment decisions and avoiding costly missteps.

Practical considerations also extend to costs beyond fund fees or brokerage commissions. Foreign transaction fees, currency conversion spreads, and custody charges can incrementally reduce net returns. Investors should seek transparent fee disclosures and compare all-in cost structures across investment vehicles. Moreover, dividend reinvestment mechanisms may differ internationally; some brokers offer automatic dividend reinvestment plans (DRIPs) for foreign securities, enhancing compounding potential, while others require manual intervention. Awareness and utilisation of such features can materially influence long-term portfolio performance.

In building a borderless REIT portfolio, investors must reconcile the tension between accessibility and control. U.S.-based global REIT funds deliver simplicity, immediate diversification, and regulatory safeguards, making them ideal for those prioritising ease and broad market exposure. Direct foreign REIT ownership appeals to seasoned investors confident in their ability to navigate complexities and capitalise on targeted opportunities. Hybrid approaches—combining pooled funds for core global exposure with selective direct investments—may offer an optimal balance, capturing broad trends while exploiting specific high-conviction ideas.

Ultimately, constructing a truly global REIT portfolio demands more than geographic diversification. It requires an integrated strategy attentive to structural nuances, regulatory environments, currency exposures, and sector dynamics. Investors who master these elements position themselves to harness the full potential of global real estate, achieving income resilience and capital appreciation beyond domestic confines. This chapter offers the frameworks, practical guidance, and critical insights essential for embarking on that journey with confidence and strategic clarity.

Chapter 9
Risk, Volatility, and the Truth About REIT Performance

REITs occupy a peculiar niche in the investment world—hailed for their income-generating potential, yet often criticised for seeming volatility. Much of this reputation, however, rests on partial understanding rather than inherent instability. The cyclical rhythms of real estate, sensitivity to interest rates, and misconceptions surrounding their beta frequently fuel a narrative that overstates REITs' culpability in market turbulence. This chapter seeks to peel back those layers, revealing a more measured perspective beneath the headlines and prevailing assumptions.

At the core of REIT performance lies a delicate interplay between macroeconomic cycles, monetary policy, and sector-specific fundamentals. Unlike conventional equities, REITs are anchored to tangible property assets whose values fluctuate with broader economic forces—interest rates being chief among them, affecting both borrowing costs and the required return investors demand. Yet the relationship is rarely straightforward. The notion that rising rates inevitably depress REIT valuations overlooks scenarios where robust rental growth, constrained supply, or strategic property management can offset such pressures. Recognising this duality is essential for investors wishing to assess REITs on their own merits, rather than through the distorting lens of market sentiment.

Equally important is dismantling the idea that REITs move in lockstep with stocks or bonds. Correlation, while a useful statistical tool, does not equate to inevitability. Historically, REITs have exhibited hybrid behaviour—sometimes diverging from equities and other times mirroring them during broad sell-offs. Examining past performance across recessions, expansions, and inflationary periods demonstrates how responses vary depending on underlying economic drivers. This nuanced understanding allows investors to position REITs strategically within a diversified portfolio, appreciating when they act as stabilising influences versus when they track broader market swings.

Yield, of course, remains the defining hallmark of REITs, but even here superficial measures can mislead. Attractive dividend yields can mask structural vulnerabilities if sustainability and payout ratios are overlooked. This chapter guides readers through analytical techniques to differentiate between dividends supported by sound earnings and those that risk eroding capital over time. Case studies illustrate instances where superficially appealing yields concealed liquidity constraints or earnings volatility, contrasting them with companies whose conservative payout policies underpinned reliable income streams and long-term compounding.

Time emerges as the ultimate hedge in REIT investing. The temptation to chase market timing is persistent yet counterproductive. Here, the emphasis is on patience, reinvestment, and harnessing the power of compounding over extended horizons. Viewing REITs through a long-term, yield-focused lens shifts the conversation from short-term speculation to durable wealth accumulation. Historical data consistently demonstrates that disciplined engagement, rather than reactionary trading, rewards investors with steady income and meaningful capital growth despite episodic volatility.

This chapter delivers a thorough, evidence-based reassessment of REIT performance, stripping away misconceptions to reveal the structural forces at play. It invites readers to reconsider volatility, correlation, and yield through an empirically informed and practically grounded lens. For the thoughtful investor, it offers a guiding framework—a compass through complexity—illuminating the enduring value REITs contribute within a diversified, income-oriented strategy.

Why REITs Get Misunderstood

Real Estate Investment Trusts (REITs) occupy a peculiar niche in financial markets—widely admired for their income generation yet often misunderstood in their risk profile and volatility. They are frequently blamed for market turbulence and volatility spikes that, upon closer inspection, they neither uniquely cause nor disproportionately exacerbate. This persistent mischaracterisation stems from a combination of REITs' inherent cyclicality, their sensitivity to interest rates, and a fundamental misunderstanding of their market beta. To truly appreciate REITs' performance characteristics, investors must disentangle these factors and approach REIT investing with nuance rather than oversimplified narratives.

REITs, by design, derive their value from physical real estate assets, and as such, their fortunes are closely tied to the cyclical rhythms of the broader economy. Economic expansions fuel demand for office space, retail outlets, industrial warehouses, and multifamily housing, driving rental growth and property valuations upward. Conversely, during recessions or downturns, vacancy rates rise, lease renewals slow, and property values may decline. This economic cyclicality naturally transmits into REIT share prices. However, unlike pure equities where earnings might fluctuate rapidly, REIT earnings and dividends tend to lag or smooth due to lease contracts and long-term tenant agreements, creating a unique risk-return profile that does not always correlate neatly with general equity markets. This lag and smoothing effect can paradoxically make REITs appear both volatile and stable depending on the investor's time horizon and market context.

Interest rate sensitivity is often cited as the chief cause of REIT volatility, but this relationship is frequently misunderstood. REITs typically carry significant debt on their balance sheets, reflecting the capital-intensive nature of real estate ownership. Rising interest rates increase borrowing costs, squeezing profit margins, and potentially reducing property valuations as capitalisation rates adjust. Yet, this dynamic oversimplifies the picture. In environments where rising rates signal strong economic growth, rent increases and property income growth can offset higher financing costs, preserving or even enhancing REIT valuations. Conversely, when rate hikes accompany economic weakness or inflation shocks, REITs may suffer more pronounced declines. Investors must recognise that interest rate impacts are context-dependent, intertwining monetary policy effects with real estate fundamentals.

The concept of beta—a measure of an asset's sensitivity to broader market movements—further complicates REIT assessment. REITs' beta values often position them somewhere between equities and bonds, but investors frequently interpret beta through a narrow equity lens. This misinterpretation leads to the false assumption that REITs inherently amplify stock market volatility, prompting reactive selling during equity downturns. In reality, REIT beta reflects a composite risk profile shaped by real estate asset class characteristics, lease contract durations, tenant quality, and capital structure. Studies show that REITs do not consistently increase portfolio volatility; rather, they can serve as a diversification tool, particularly when considered alongside traditional equity and fixed income assets. The failure to contextualise beta within REITs' hybrid asset status fosters misconceptions about their risk contribution.

Market narratives exacerbate these misunderstandings. During periods of financial stress or rapid interest rate changes, REITs often experience sharp price corrections, attracting outsized attention and becoming scapegoats for broader market volatility. Media coverage and investor sentiment can amplify these movements beyond what fundamentals justify, triggering feedback loops of selling and reinforcing the perception of REITs as volatile or speculative investments. This phenomenon underscores the critical role of behavioural finance in shaping asset class reputations—where perception can diverge significantly from economic reality.

Real-world examples illustrate these complexities. The 2008 global financial crisis saw REIT prices plummet as credit markets froze and property valuations collapsed, validating their cyclical risk exposure. However, the subsequent decade of low interest rates and steady economic growth propelled REITs to deliver robust returns and consistent dividends, challenging their volatility stereotype. More recently, the rapid interest rate increases in 2022 triggered significant REIT price declines, yet those with strong tenant fundamentals and conservative leverage weathered the storm better than others. These instances affirm that volatility is not a universal REIT trait but a function of specific economic and financial contexts, portfolio construction, and management quality.

Investors must also contend with the structural features of REITs that influence volatility perceptions. Dividend payout mandates require REITs to distribute a substantial portion of taxable income as dividends, which can constrain retained earnings for reinvestment and increase dependence on external capital markets. This characteristic can magnify price sensitivity to changes in financing conditions and investor appetite for income-generating assets. Yet, this high distribution rate is also the source of REITs' appeal for income-focused investors. Understanding this duality is vital to appreciating why REIT prices can react sharply to dividend yield fluctuations without necessarily reflecting fundamental deterioration.

Ultimately, dispelling the myths around REIT volatility requires embracing a comprehensive view that integrates economic cycles, interest rate environments, and asset-specific factors. It demands moving beyond simplistic beta comparisons and recognising REITs' hybrid status as both equity and real estate instruments. By doing so, investors can better calibrate expectations, harness REITs' income potential, and strategically deploy them within diversified portfolios. Far from being mere sources of market volatility, REITs emerge as complex, multifaceted assets whose risk and return characteristics merit informed, nuanced consideration rather than reflexive blame.

Correlation Isn't Destiny

Correlation often serves as the shorthand by which investors attempt to grasp the behaviour of asset classes in relation to one another. At first glance, real estate investment trusts (REITs) seem to fit neatly within the broader equity universe, frequently displaying moderate to high correlations with stock markets. However, to regard correlation as destiny — the inevitable co-movement of returns — is to overlook the nuanced interplay of economic forces, market structure, and sector-specific dynamics that shape REIT performance across varied macroeconomic environments. Understanding why correlation alone cannot define REITs' role in a portfolio demands a deeper examination of how they interact with stocks, bonds, and underlying real estate assets under shifting economic conditions.

At the most fundamental level, REITs straddle multiple investment categories. They are equity securities, yet their cash flows derive from physical real estate — an inherently illiquid, tangible asset class. This dual nature engenders complex relationships with other asset classes.

Over long periods, REITs have exhibited positive correlations with stocks, often cited in the range of 0.5 to 0.8, reflecting shared sensitivity to growth prospects, market sentiment, and broader capital flows. Yet, these numbers belie the cyclical and economic specificity underpinning REIT returns. During periods of economic expansion, for instance, rising corporate profits and consumer spending typically support both equities and commercial real estate fundamentals, fostering alignment in performance. Conversely, during recessions or financial crises, divergences emerge sharply as credit conditions, lease renewals, and occupancy rates dictate REIT earnings in ways stocks do not.

Interest rates inject further complexity. REITs tend to be more sensitive to interest rate changes than broad equity indices, owing to their capital-intensive business models and reliance on debt financing. When central banks tighten monetary policy, bond yields rise, making fixed income instruments more attractive relative to dividend-paying equities, including REITs. The resulting investor rotation can temporarily depress REIT valuations even as the underlying properties maintain or grow income streams. Thus, in rising rate environments, correlations between REITs and bonds may strengthen, countering the notion that REITs always move in tandem with stocks. Such dynamics underscore why simple correlation measures mask the conditional dependencies dictated by macroeconomic factors.

Examining REITs relative to traditional real estate further clarifies their unique profile. Private real estate investments typically show low correlation with public equities because of appraisal-based valuations, illiquidity, and longer investment horizons. REITs, as publicly traded instruments, incorporate market pricing and sentiment, resulting in higher short-term volatility and correlations with equity markets. However, they provide greater transparency, liquidity, and accessibility. The divergence between public REIT performance and private real estate returns during market dislocations illustrates that while related, these asset classes respond to distinct signals and investor behaviours. Notably, REITs often lead shifts in real estate cycles, reflecting investor expectations ahead of slower-moving private markets.

Geographical and sectoral diversification within REITs further complicates correlation assumptions. Industrial and logistics REITs, driven by e-commerce trends, have experienced robust growth relatively independent of broader equity movements. Conversely, retail REITs remain vulnerable to secular pressures affecting consumer foot traffic, often correlating more closely with consumer discretionary stocks during downturns. Healthcare REITs, with long-term lease structures tied to demographic shifts, may demonstrate different sensitivity to economic shocks. International REITs add currency risk and differing regulatory environments, creating layers of complexity beyond domestic correlations. Therefore, the heterogeneity within the REIT universe dilutes any simplistic categorisation based solely on correlation coefficients.

Real-world events reinforce these conceptual points. The global financial crisis of 2008 saw REITs decline sharply in lockstep with equities and credit markets, yet the recovery phase revealed the resilience of certain REIT sectors as economic fundamentals improved. The COVID-19 pandemic disrupted retail and hospitality REITs disproportionately, while industrial and data centre REITs surged, diverging markedly from the broad equity market. Interest rate volatility in recent years again demonstrated how shifts in monetary policy can transiently decouple REIT performance from traditional equity benchmarks. Such episodes illustrate that correlation fluctuates with time and circumstance rather than serving as a fixed investment axiom.

From a portfolio construction standpoint, this nuanced understanding is critical. Investors seeking diversification benefits from REITs must look beyond historical correlation metrics and assess how REITs behave in various economic scenarios, under different inflation regimes, and amidst changing interest rate landscapes. The inclusion of REITs may reduce portfolio volatility and enhance income generation if selected with an awareness of these conditional relationships. Relying solely on correlation risks misallocation and missed opportunities to harness REITs' distinctive cash flow profiles and inflation hedging characteristics.

Ultimately, recognising that correlation isn't destiny demands intellectual humility and a willingness to embrace complexity. It invites investors to integrate macroeconomic insight, sectoral analysis, and strategic foresight into their REIT allocation decisions. This approach transcends simplistic statistical measures and positions REITs not merely as equity proxies but as a versatile asset class whose performance contours shift with the evolving economic terrain. Understanding these dynamics empowers investors to navigate volatility, capitalise on structural real estate trends, and construct portfolios robust against the vagaries of markets.

Correlation offers a starting point, not a conclusion, in deciphering REIT performance. Approached with rigor and nuance, it becomes a tool for discerning REITs' true portfolio role — one defined by conditional behaviours rather than immutable fate. This perspective equips investors with the clarity to deploy REITs strategically, optimising risk-adjusted returns across economic cycles rather than succumbing to oversimplified myths about co-movement.

Reading Between the Yields

The allure of a high dividend yield is undeniable, especially within the realm of Real Estate Investment Trusts (REITs), where consistent income streams often take centre stage for investors. Yet, beneath the surface of headline yields lies a complex interplay of financial health, operational sustainability, and strategic capital management that demands careful scrutiny. Reading between the yields is less about chasing headline percentages and more about discerning the underlying quality and longevity of those payments—a skill essential to navigating REIT investing with both prudence and sophistication.

To understand dividend sustainability in REITs, one must begin with the payout ratio, a fundamental metric revealing the proportion of earnings distributed to shareholders. Unlike many conventional companies, REITs are legally mandated to distribute at least 90% of their taxable income as dividends to maintain their tax-advantaged status. This legal requirement sets the stage for inherently high payout ratios within the sector, often exceeding 80% to 100%. However, a high payout ratio in isolation does not guarantee dividend safety; it can also signal financial stress or limited retained earnings to fund growth and buffer economic shocks. Thus, a critical distinction emerges between a high yield and a *healthy* yield—where health encompasses coverage, growth potential, and balance sheet robustness.

Consider the example of two REITs delivering a similar 7% yield. The first maintains a payout ratio near 90%, underpinned by stable funds from operations (FFO) and prudent leverage, indicating sustainable income and sound capital allocation. The second, however, exhibits a payout ratio exceeding 110%, raising red flags about dividend financing through debt or asset sales—unsustainable tactics that may precipitate dividend cuts. This contrast exemplifies why investors must dig deeper, evaluating not just the yield but the *source* and *stability* of dividend distributions.

Funds From Operations, or FFO, serves as a superior earnings proxy for REITs, adjusting net income for non-cash depreciation and amortisation on real estate assets—items that, unlike other industries, do not reflect cash outflows. FFO more accurately captures operational cash generation, providing a clearer picture of dividend coverage. Yet even FFO warrants scrutiny: variations such as Adjusted FFO (AFFO) further refine cash flow metrics by accounting for recurring capital expenditures necessary to maintain asset quality. An REIT with a strong AFFO coverage ratio over its dividend payment reveals a sustainable dividend framework, while a widening gap between dividends and AFFO signals caution.

Beyond payout ratios and cash flow, leverage and balance sheet strength critically influence dividend sustainability. REITs operate capital-intensive businesses requiring debt financing to acquire and manage properties. High leverage can amplify returns in favourable markets but also magnify risk during downturns. Credit metrics such as debt-to-EBITDA and interest coverage ratios contextualise dividend risk; a REIT burdened with excessive debt relative to cash flow may be forced to slash dividends to preserve solvency. Thus, *assessing financial resilience* alongside dividend metrics offers a comprehensive view of sustainability.

Moreover, sector-specific dynamics affect dividend reliability. For instance, healthcare REITs often benefit from long-term leases with stable tenants, translating to predictable income streams and resilient dividends. Conversely, retail REITs face evolving consumer behaviours and tenant bankruptcies, introducing volatility that can imperil dividends despite superficially attractive yields. Investors must consider these idiosyncrasies in conjunction with quantitative metrics, appreciating how industry trends and lease structures shape dividend prospects.

Market conditions also modulate the dividend narrative. Rising interest rates typically pressure high-dividend sectors like REITs, as competing income sources become more attractive, compressing valuations and yields. Yet, some REITs may exhibit pricing power or inflation-linked leases that support dividend growth, underscoring the importance of distinguishing between transient market reactions and fundamental dividend health. A high yield born of share price decline may tempt investors, but without solid coverage and growth, it risks being a yield trap.

Dividend growth potential complements current yield in evaluating dividend quality. A REIT with a moderate yield but consistent dividend growth may outperform a higher-yielding but stagnant or shrinking peer over the long term. Dividend reinvestment amplifies compounding effects, reinforcing why a *forward-looking* perspective on dividend sustainability trumps static yield snapshots.

Finally, ethical considerations and corporate governance practices influence dividend integrity. Transparent disclosure, prudent capital allocation, and management's commitment to balanced growth versus payout strategies affect investor confidence. REITs that prioritise long-term stakeholder value through disciplined dividend policies and sustainable growth models distinguish themselves as trustworthy income sources.

Reading between the yields demands synthesising quantitative analysis with qualitative judgement—understanding the interplay of payout ratios, cash flow metrics, leverage, sectoral dynamics, market environment, and corporate governance. It is this layered analysis that transforms raw dividend numbers into actionable investment insight, enabling investors to discern truly sustainable income streams from ephemeral allure. Mastery of these concepts equips investors to navigate the REIT landscape with clarity, resilience, and strategic foresight.

Time as the Ultimate Hedge

Time emerges as the most potent ally in Real Estate Investment Trust (REIT) investing, a truth often overshadowed by the allure of market timing and short-term speculation. While the temptation to precisely predict market movements is perennial, history and data collectively attest that patience and long-term commitment decisively outperform attempts to time entry or exit points. This subchapter unpacks why *time itself* constitutes the ultimate hedge for REIT investors, and how the compounding effects of reinvested dividends, income stability, and gradual capital appreciation coalesce to build enduring wealth.

REITs, by their very nature, are designed to distribute regular income to shareholders. Unlike typical equities where dividend payments may fluctuate or be suspended, REITs are legally obligated to pay out the vast majority of their taxable earnings as dividends. This structural feature makes them uniquely income-focused investments. Consequently, *time allows investors to harness the power of compounding income*, where dividends received are reinvested to purchase additional shares, which in turn generate more dividends. This virtuous cycle magnifies total returns substantially over extended periods, transforming what may initially appear as modest yields into substantial wealth accumulation.

Consider empirical evidence from decades of REIT performance studies. Investors who held diversified REIT portfolios over 10, 20, or 30 years consistently outperformed those who attempted short-term tactical trades. Volatility and cyclical downturns—common in the real estate sector—are smoothed by holding through full market cycles. Market corrections often present opportunities for additional investments at lower prices, enhancing future yield-on-cost. Conversely, attempts to avoid downturns through timing often lead to missing rebounds and compounding returns, underscoring the futility of speculative trading in this asset class.

One must also appreciate how the time horizon interacts with dividend sustainability. REITs with disciplined capital management and robust balance sheets are better positioned to maintain and grow dividends over time, even through economic turbulence. This resilience further reinforces the argument that *investing duration rather than timing* is key; investors who commit to a long-term horizon reap the benefits of dividend growth alongside capital appreciation, both of which are less visible in shorter holding periods.

The concept of dollar-cost averaging dovetails elegantly with the long-term thesis. By investing fixed sums at regular intervals, investors systematically buy more shares when prices are low and fewer when prices are high. This reduces the risk of ill-timed lump-sum investments and complements the compounding mechanism. Dollar-cost averaging transforms investing from a speculative gamble to a disciplined strategy that leverages market fluctuations rather than succumbing to them.

However, embracing time as the ultimate hedge also requires a corresponding mindset shift. The emotional volatility associated with dividend fluctuations or share price corrections must be tempered by a strategic vision prioritising cumulative wealth over immediate gratification. This entails recognising that dividend cuts or market dips, while unsettling, are often temporary setbacks in a longer narrative of growth. Moreover, the patience required can only be cultivated through rigorous due diligence—selecting REITs with strong fundamentals, transparent management, and sustainable payout policies.

Another dimension of time's importance is revealed through the tax efficiency of long-term holding. Frequent trading of REIT shares can trigger tax liabilities on capital gains, eroding net returns. By contrast, patient investors who reinvest dividends within tax-advantaged accounts or hold shares for longer durations reduce tax drag, further enhancing compounding outcomes.

It is instructive to reflect on historical episodes where REIT markets faced sharp corrections—such as the 2008 financial crisis or the pandemic-induced downturn in 2020. Investors who maintained or increased exposure during these periods experienced accelerated recovery and gains, while those who retreated locked in losses. These cases vividly demonstrate that *time absorbs volatility and amplifies opportunity*, a principle underpinning the superiority of a long-term investment horizon.

Finally, this approach aligns REIT investing with foundational principles of value investing and wealth creation espoused by financial luminaries. The incremental, sustained growth generated through income reinvestment and capital appreciation transcends short-lived market trends and speculative noise. It rewards discipline, informed patience, and strategic foresight—the hallmarks of enduring investment success.

In essence, the passage of time smooths volatility, magnifies income through compounding, enhances dividend growth capture, and mitigates tax impacts, making it the paramount hedge in REIT investing. Recognising and embracing this fact redefines how investors approach REITs—not as vehicles for quick profits but as engines for long-term, resilient wealth accumulation. This subchapter guides readers to internalise time as a strategic advantage and equips them to navigate the complexities of REIT markets with confidence and clarity.

Chapter 10
The Laws That Shape REITs—and Your Freedom

The emergence of Real Estate Investment Trusts (REITs) cannot be disentangled from the legal and fiscal frameworks that both birthed and continue to shape them. To grasp why REITs exist—and why they remain relevant—one must examine the delicate interplay of legislation, economic imperatives, and public policy. At its heart, the REIT model was designed to democratise real estate investment, anchored by a stringent distribution requirement: at least 90% of taxable income must be disbursed as dividends. This legal mandate not only ensures predictable income for investors but also aligns the interests of all stakeholders, cultivating transparency and confidence. This chapter undertakes a detailed exploration of the regulatory structures that define REITs, highlighting how these rules delineate investor rights and the operational latitude of these vehicles.

The regulatory environment for REITs is far from homogenous. While the United States pioneered the model with a clearly defined legal framework, international legislation varies widely, presenting both opportunities and pitfalls for global investors. These differences influence accessibility, yield characteristics, and the scope of permissible activities within each market. Navigating this complex mosaic requires a keen understanding of how local and cross-border rules can either constrain or amplify returns. This chapter examines these global variations, clarifying how regulation shapes the very character and potential of REITs worldwide.

Taxation is a particularly intricate dimension. REIT dividends occupy a unique niche within tax codes, reflecting their pass-through nature. In the U.S., for example, REIT distributions are treated differently from ordinary corporate dividends, with consequences for personal investors and retirement accounts alike. Abroad, withholding taxes and bilateral agreements add further complexity, subtly influencing net returns if unconsidered. This chapter demystifies these nuances, arming readers with the knowledge to optimise international portfolios while avoiding hidden pitfalls.

Beyond legal and fiscal mechanics, REITs fulfil a wider societal function. They do more than channel private wealth; they serve as vehicles for funding critical infrastructure, affordable housing, healthcare facilities, and other public necessities. Viewed in this light, REITs operate at the intersection of private capital and social utility. The laws that govern them thus carry a dual responsibility: safeguarding investors while enabling the flow of funds into sectors that underpin societal and economic well-being.

Examining these regulations is far from a dry exercise. This chapter offers a critical lens for understanding the foundational forces governing REITs, marrying legal analysis with practical insights and philosophical reflection. It encourages readers to see REITs not merely as investment vehicles but as dynamic entities operating within a structured ecosystem that both limits and enables possibilities.

Through comparative studies and real-world examples, the chapter explores the ongoing dialogue between regulation and innovation in the REIT space. Legislative amendments, tax reforms, and market evolution continually reshape the landscape, demanding vigilance and informed engagement from investors. Additionally, it prompts reflection on the ethical and social dimensions inherent in REIT investing, challenging readers to consider the broader impact of their capital decisions on communities and economies.

Ultimately, this chapter provides a comprehensive guide to the legal foundations of REITs, revealing the balance between regulation and freedom that defines the investor experience. By understanding these dynamics, readers are better equipped to navigate the REIT landscape with intellectual rigour and strategic insight, appreciating how legal architecture both protects and empowers those participating in the evolving world of real estate investment trusts.

Why REITs Exist (and Keep Existing)

The Real Estate Investment Trust (REIT) stands as one of the most innovative financial instruments of the twentieth century, yet its existence is not a mere accident of market evolution. Rather, REITs emerged as a deliberate legislative and tax-engineered response to a very specific challenge: how to open real estate investing to the broader public while preserving tax efficiency and investor protections. Their survival and ongoing relevance hinge upon a legal framework designed to balance the interests of investors, regulators, and the economy itself. Central to this framework is the oft-cited but frequently misunderstood *90% distribution rule*—a requirement that REITs distribute at least ninety percent of their taxable income to shareholders in the form of dividends. This article delves deeply into the origins and implications of REIT legislation, explaining how the legal and tax structures that underpin these entities not only safeguard investors but also maintain the REIT's enduring presence in global capital markets.

The genesis of REITs traces back to the early 1960s in the United States, a period when access to real estate was largely limited to institutional investors or wealthy individuals capable of direct property ownership. Recognising real estate's potential as a stable income source, lawmakers sought to democratise this asset class without undermining its tax advantages. Prior to REIT legislation, real estate investments through traditional corporate structures suffered from *double taxation*—once at the corporate level on earnings, and again at the investor level upon distribution of dividends. This inefficiency dissuaded many potential investors and constrained capital flows into real estate development and maintenance. The solution: create a corporate entity exempt from federal income tax provided it adhered to certain operational mandates, chief among them the 90% distribution rule.

This distribution requirement serves a dual purpose. First, it ensures that the bulk of earnings generated by REITs flows directly to investors, establishing a predictable and reliable income stream. This is particularly attractive to income-focused investors such as retirees or those seeking regular cash flow. Second, by mandating near-total payout of taxable income, the rule prevents the accumulation of earnings within the REIT that could otherwise be reinvested without shareholder approval, thus fostering transparency and accountability. *Investors are not left in the dark about the fate of profits*, as REITs must maintain rigorous reporting standards aligned with their regulatory obligations.

However, the 90% distribution mandate is not merely an arbitrary figure; it reflects a carefully considered trade-off between taxation and operational flexibility. By obliging REITs to distribute most of their income, the government essentially exchanges tax exemption for income transparency and shareholder priority. This contrasts sharply with traditional corporations that may retain earnings to fund growth, but in doing so, invite layered taxation. Consequently, REITs operate as "pass-through" entities for tax purposes—profits flow through to investors who then bear the individual tax burden. This structural characteristic is a fundamental reason why REITs attract income-oriented investors, yet it simultaneously shapes their capital management strategies, often limiting aggressive reinvestment.

The regulatory framework governing REITs extends beyond distribution rules to include asset composition, income sources, and organisational structure. For example, to qualify as a REIT, at least 75% of a company's assets must be invested in real estate, cash, or government securities, and at least 75% of gross income must derive from real estate-related sources such as rents or mortgage interest. These restrictions are designed to *preserve the REIT's real estate focus*, preventing mission drift into unrelated sectors that might dilute the investment's intended risk and return profile. Additionally, REITs must be structured as taxable corporations, managed by a board of directors or trustees, and must have a minimum of 100 shareholders, ensuring broad ownership and professional governance.

Critics sometimes argue that the mandatory dividend payout limits REITs' ability to pursue growth opportunities, especially in capital-intensive sectors such as logistics or technology-infused real estate. Yet, this critique overlooks the sophisticated capital markets infrastructure REITs access to fund expansion without relying solely on retained earnings. By issuing equity or debt, REITs tap into a global pool of capital, demonstrating how *the 90% distribution rule does not inhibit growth but rather redirects how growth is financed.* This mechanism reinforces the alignment between investor expectations and corporate strategy, as shareholders explicitly understand the trade-off between immediate income and potential capital appreciation.

The legal and tax origins of REITs have also influenced investor protections. Because REITs operate under stringent regulatory scrutiny, they are subject to comprehensive disclosure requirements, including regular financial reporting and governance mandates. This regulatory oversight reduces information asymmetry—a common source of risk in real estate investments—and offers investors transparency often absent in private property ventures. Furthermore, the structural insistence on diversified ownership and board oversight mitigates conflicts of interest and opportunistic management, enhancing the overall stability of REITs as investment vehicles.

Importantly, the REIT model's success in the United States has spurred its adoption worldwide, albeit with adaptations to local tax regimes and legal frameworks. Countries such as Singapore, Japan, and Australia have developed REIT structures that reflect their unique economic, fiscal, and legal contexts but maintain the core principle of tax-efficient real estate investment accessible to a broad investor base. These international variants confirm that the fundamental balance REIT legislation strikes—between investor protection, tax efficiency, and market accessibility—is not a mere regulatory artifact but a resilient model adaptable to diverse markets.

Reflecting on the 90% distribution rule's protective function reveals deeper ethical and economic considerations. By mandating near-complete income distribution, REITs contribute to market discipline, discouraging excessive risk-taking by management and promoting shareholder returns as the primary corporate objective. This legal safeguard aligns with the public interest by channelling capital into income-producing real estate assets, which in turn support housing, commercial development, and infrastructure essential for economic vitality. Thus, REITs emerge not only as investment tools but as vehicles of economic utility, fostering capital formation while embedding investor safeguards.

Nevertheless, it is crucial to recognise the limitations and challenges inherent in the REIT structure. The mandatory payout policy may result in tax inefficiencies for investors in higher tax brackets, and the reliance on external financing can expose REITs to market volatility and interest rate fluctuations. Additionally, as real estate markets evolve—incorporating more technology-driven assets and innovative financing models—the rigidity of traditional REIT rules may necessitate legislative adaptations to sustain relevance and competitiveness. These tensions highlight the ongoing dialogue between regulation and innovation, reminding investors that the legal framework, while protective, is not static but subject to continuous refinement.

In sum, the raison d'être of REITs lies in a carefully calibrated legal and tax design that democratizes access to real estate income, ensures investor protection through mandated distributions, and balances growth ambitions with fiscal discipline. This structure has endured because it aligns the interests of regulators, investors, and the broader economy, creating a transparent and efficient conduit for real estate investment. Understanding the *why* behind REITs is essential not only for appreciating their historical success but for navigating their future evolution amid changing economic and regulatory landscapes. The 90% distribution rule, far from a mere regulatory hurdle, is the cornerstone of a model that continues to deliver investor security and opportunity in equal measure.

Regulation vs. Opportunity

Regulation is the silent architect shaping the contours of real estate investment trusts (REITs) across the globe, dictating who can invest, how returns are structured, and the risks investors must shoulder. Yet, this regulatory landscape is far from uniform. Legal frameworks vary widely between countries, creating a complex mosaic where the same investment vehicle—REITs—assumes markedly different characteristics depending on jurisdiction. For international investors, understanding these regulatory nuances is not merely academic; it is a prerequisite for navigating the delicate balance between risk and opportunity in global real estate markets. This article examines how divergent laws influence REIT accessibility, yield profiles, and risk exposure, revealing that regulation is both a gatekeeper and a catalyst—simultaneously constraining and enabling investment potential.

The regulatory environment governing REITs functions as a dual-edged instrument. On one hand, it provides the structural integrity necessary for investor protection, ensuring transparency, income distribution, and adherence to real estate-focused activities. On the other, it imposes restrictions that can limit market access, capital raising flexibility, and operational freedom. The United States offers a quintessential example: its pioneering REIT legislation mandates a minimum of 100 shareholders, restricts non-qualifying asset exposure to 25%, and requires distribution of at least 90% of taxable income. These rules have crafted a robust, liquid market that balances investor safeguards with growth potential. However, for non-U.S. investors, such rules also mean navigating the complexities of foreign tax treatment, currency risk, and differing market dynamics.

Contrast this with Singapore, a jurisdiction lauded for its efficient REIT framework but markedly different in approach. Singaporean REITs (S-REITs) benefit from a corporate tax exemption on income distributed to unitholders, promoting high dividend yields attractive to yield-seeking investors. Yet, stringent ownership and investment restrictions—such as limits on single-asset exposure—shape portfolio construction differently than their American counterparts. Furthermore, Singapore imposes withholding taxes on foreign investors, directly impacting net returns. Here, regulation fosters a market characterised by stability and yield reliability but with distinct cost considerations and risk exposures shaped by its regulatory DNA.

Europe's REIT ecosystem exemplifies fragmentation, reflecting diverse legal traditions and economic priorities. The United Kingdom's REIT regime, introduced in 2007, emphasises transparency and dividend distribution similar to the U.S., yet allows a broader range of qualifying assets, including certain infrastructure investments. This flexibility has catalysed innovative REIT models blending real estate with infrastructure assets, appealing to investors seeking growth and diversification. Conversely, Germany's REIT system enforces stricter asset and income tests, limiting REITs primarily to commercial real estate and imposing capital gain tax considerations. These variations mean that an international investor cannot assume homogeneity in risk or opportunity simply by virtue of investing in a European REIT.

Emerging markets add further complexity and potential reward. In regions like Latin America and parts of Asia, nascent REIT regulations are often evolving, creating both opportunity and uncertainty. For instance, Brazil's real estate funds (FIIs) have seen regulatory enhancements aimed at improving liquidity and investor protection, yet political and economic volatility remains a significant factor influencing returns. In India, Real Estate Investment Trusts only recently gained legal footing, and regulatory frameworks continue to develop, resulting in constrained market size but significant growth potential. The juxtaposition of opportunity and risk here underscores the need for a nuanced regulatory understanding—where the promise of outsized returns is tempered by governance and market stability concerns.

Regulation also directly influences yield characteristics and investor risk exposure. Jurisdictions that enforce high dividend distribution requirements often produce REITs with reliable income streams but limited capacity for internal growth, compelling reliance on external capital markets. Countries with lenient payout mandates may exhibit greater capital appreciation but heightened volatility. Moreover, investor protections such as disclosure requirements and governance standards vary, impacting the transparency and predictability of returns. Investors must therefore carefully assess how local regulatory frameworks shape the fundamental economics of REITs, beyond headline yield figures.

An illustrative example can be found in the comparative volatility profiles of REITs across different markets. U.S. REITs, traded on deep and liquid exchanges, tend to exhibit lower liquidity risk and more efficient price discovery, albeit with sensitivity to interest rate shifts. In contrast, REITs in smaller or less mature markets may trade infrequently, exposing investors to liquidity premiums and valuation uncertainties. Regulatory constraints on foreign ownership in certain countries further complicate access and exit strategies, increasing implicit transaction costs and risk profiles for international investors.

Taxation intersects crucially with regulation, adding a further layer of complexity. The treatment of REIT dividends—often classified as ordinary income rather than qualified dividends—affects after-tax returns. Countries differ in withholding tax rates applied to foreign investors, and some impose additional layers of taxation, such as capital gains tax on REIT share sales or estate taxes. For global investors, these fiscal nuances materially alter the attractiveness of REIT investments and can diminish apparent yield advantages if not properly accounted for in portfolio construction and asset allocation decisions.

Yet, regulation should not be viewed solely as a barrier. In many cases, it creates opportunity by establishing credibility and investor confidence. Well-regulated REIT markets tend to attract institutional capital, foster secondary market development, and enable access to lower-cost financing. This virtuous cycle enhances REIT liquidity and growth potential. Moreover, regulatory innovation—such as the introduction of sustainability reporting requirements or expanded asset eligibility—can unlock new sectors and investment themes, positioning REITs as dynamic instruments responsive to evolving economic and social priorities.

The challenge for the international investor lies in synthesising this regulatory complexity into a coherent investment framework. Access decisions must weigh not only legal permissibility but also operational practicality, market maturity, and alignment with strategic objectives. Some investors may prefer the relative safety and standardisation of established markets like the U.S. or Singapore, while others may embrace emerging market REITs for growth and diversification, accepting greater regulatory and political risk. The key is to understand that regulation is a lens through which opportunity must be viewed—not a fixed constraint but a variable factor shaping risk, return, and portfolio construction.

In summary, the global regulatory environment for REITs presents a spectrum of configurations, each imparting unique implications for investor access, yield expectations, and risk exposure. International investors equipped with a deep understanding of these regulatory distinctions can navigate the subtle interplay between protection and opportunity, turning legal complexity into a strategic advantage. Recognising that regulation is neither inherently restrictive nor permissive—but context-dependent—empowers investors to make informed decisions that align with their risk tolerance, investment horizon, and return objectives. This delicate balance underscores the essential truth: in global REIT investing, regulatory insight is as critical as market analysis for unlocking sustainable value.

Taxation and the Hidden Costs

Taxation is an often overlooked but profoundly influential dimension of Real Estate Investment Trust (REIT) investing, shaping not only net returns but also the strategic decisions investors make across borders and account types. While REITs attract capital with their promise of steady dividends and capital appreciation, the tax environment that envelops these returns—complex, multi-jurisdictional, and frequently opaque—can significantly erode investor wealth if not properly understood. This chapter peels back the layers of U.S. and global tax regimes as they apply to REIT dividends, retirement accounts, foreign withholding, and the pass-through nature of REITs. It reveals the hidden costs embedded in seemingly straightforward income streams and underscores why a sophisticated grasp of taxation is indispensable for both individual and institutional investors who seek to optimise after-tax outcomes without falling prey to costly surprises.

Central to the tax discourse surrounding REITs is their unique status as pass-through entities. Unlike conventional corporations that pay corporate income tax before distributing dividends, REITs are structured to avoid double taxation by passing most of their taxable income directly to shareholders. The U.S. REIT model, governed by the Internal Revenue Code, mandates that REITs distribute at least 90% of taxable income annually to maintain their tax-advantaged status. While this mechanism preserves capital efficiency at the corporate level, it transforms the nature of dividends into what is effectively ordinary income for recipients, typically taxed at higher rates than qualified dividends. This distinction sets the stage for one of the primary "hidden costs" investors must navigate: the tax drag associated with REIT dividend income, which can materially diminish after-tax yield compared to other equity income streams.

Moreover, REIT dividends may contain multiple components—ordinary income, return of capital, and capital gains—each subject to differing tax treatments. For instance, a portion of distributions might be classified as return of capital, which reduces the investor's cost basis and defers taxation until the eventual sale of shares. While this can be beneficial in postponing tax liabilities, it complicates portfolio accounting and can lead to unexpectedly large capital gains taxes if cost basis adjustments are not meticulously tracked. Sophisticated investors and portfolio managers employ detailed tax lot accounting and may leverage tax-aware software to monitor these nuances, a complexity that underscores the criticality of tax literacy in REIT investing.

The interplay between REIT taxation and retirement accounts introduces another layer of strategic consideration. In the U.S., holding REITs in tax-advantaged accounts such as Individual Retirement Accounts (IRAs) or 401(k) plans can shield dividends from immediate taxation, allowing dividends to compound more efficiently over time. However, this sheltering is nuanced by factors such as Unrelated Business Taxable Income (UBTI) and, in some cases, Unrelated Debt-Financed Income (UDFI), which can trigger tax liabilities within these tax-exempt vehicles when leveraged REIT investments are involved. While the average retail investor may never encounter these complexities, institutional investors and high-net-worth individuals must exercise vigilance, as failure to account for UBTI and UDFI can erode the expected tax benefits and introduce compliance risks.

When stepping beyond domestic borders, the taxation of REIT dividends becomes even more labyrinthine. Foreign withholding taxes, levied at the source country before dividends reach the investor, can substantially reduce net income. These withholding rates vary widely—from negligible in some tax treaties to upwards of 30% in jurisdictions lacking bilateral agreements with the investor's home country. Although many investors can recoup some of these losses through foreign tax credits, the administrative burden and timing of such recoveries can be onerous. Additionally, differing classification of REIT income, currency translation effects, and local tax filing obligations contribute to a taxation landscape that demands specialised expertise or trusted advisory relationships.

International REIT investors also confront challenges relating to tax transparency and information exchange standards. The advent of global initiatives such as the OECD's Common Reporting Standard (CRS) and the Foreign Account Tax Compliance Act (FATCA) have tightened disclosure requirements, aiming to curb tax evasion but also increasing compliance costs and procedural complexity for investors and fund managers alike. These regulations implicitly raise the "hidden costs" of global REIT investing, necessitating careful evaluation of service providers, custodians, and brokers to ensure both tax compliance and efficient reporting.

An illustrative example can be drawn from Canadian REITs, which, unlike their U.S. counterparts, are often structured as publicly traded trusts with different tax profiles. Canadian investors typically benefit from favourable dividend tax credits on eligible dividends, enhancing after-tax yields, whereas U.S. investors in Canadian REITs face withholding taxes without the benefit of these credits, unless mitigated by treaty provisions. This dynamic underscores how nationality and domicile critically influence tax outcomes and can dictate portfolio allocation decisions beyond traditional financial metrics.

Equally important is the impact of taxation on REIT fund structures, such as mutual funds and exchange-traded funds (ETFs) that hold REITs. These pooled vehicles introduce an additional layer of taxation at the fund level, including capital gains distributions and potential embedded gains from portfolio turnover. For tax-sensitive investors, understanding how fund managers' trading strategies, distribution policies, and jurisdictional domiciles affect tax efficiency is essential to achieving intended after-tax returns. Funds domiciled in jurisdictions with investor-friendly tax treaties and transparent withholding procedures tend to offer superior net yield profiles, reinforcing the need for due diligence beyond headline expense ratios.

Taxation also influences behavioural aspects of investing. The prospect of high tax bills can deter dividend reinvestment or precipitate premature selling, which undermines the long-term compounding advantage intrinsic to REITs. Wise investors adopt strategies such as tax-loss harvesting, strategic asset location (allocating REITs to tax-advantaged accounts), and mindful withdrawal sequencing to mitigate these effects. The narrative around REITs must therefore encompass not just their operational and market characteristics, but also a disciplined, tax-conscious approach to portfolio management.

In synthesising these considerations, it becomes evident that taxation and hidden costs are integral to understanding REIT investment returns—not incidental footnotes but central variables shaping investor outcomes. The discipline of navigating U.S. and global tax treatments, retirement account intricacies, foreign withholding layers, and pass-through implications transforms REIT investing from a simplistic pursuit of yield to a sophisticated endeavour demanding both financial and fiscal acumen. Investors who master this domain position themselves not only to preserve capital but to unlock the full potential of REITs as instruments of income generation and portfolio diversification in an increasingly complex global landscape.

REITs as a Public Good

Real Estate Investment Trusts (REITs) occupy a unique position in modern finance, often viewed primarily as vehicles for income generation and portfolio diversification. Yet this perspective underestimates their broader societal role. Beyond delivering dividends and capital appreciation to investors, REITs function as critical financiers of public infrastructure, affordable housing, healthcare facilities, and essential community services. This dual identity—both as investment instruments and as contributors to public welfare—positions REITs at a vital intersection of capital markets and social impact, challenging investors to consider not only returns but also the tangible value these structures provide to society.

The architectural foundation of REITs, rooted in pooling capital to acquire and manage real estate assets at scale, inherently aligns with addressing large-scale societal needs. Historically, real estate development and infrastructure projects have required enormous upfront capital and long time horizons that few individual investors could bear alone. REITs democratise this access, aggregating resources to fund projects that underpin cities and regions—office parks that house businesses, apartment complexes that provide shelter, hospitals that deliver care, and data centres that support the digital economy. By channeling capital into these tangible assets, REITs facilitate the creation and maintenance of essential services that benefit millions, often with the implicit approval of public authorities and regulatory bodies.

One illuminating example lies in the healthcare sector. Healthcare REITs have emerged as substantial owners of medical office buildings, senior living facilities, and hospitals. Their investment not only supports the physical infrastructure essential for delivering health services but also enhances operational efficiencies by enabling specialised property management and capital improvements. This impact transcends financial metrics; it affects patient outcomes, accessibility, and the overall quality of care. For instance, the proliferation of REIT-owned senior housing complexes responds to demographic trends and social needs, offering professionally managed environments that address the complexities of ageing populations. The alignment of investor capital with social imperatives exemplifies how REITs act as enablers of public good.

Affordable housing constitutes another critical frontier where REITs' role as public benefactors is evident. The persistent shortage of affordable rental units in many urban centres has attracted increasing REIT participation, both from publicly traded entities and private real estate funds structured as REITs. While market incentives drive profitability, the sheer scale of these investments contributes to mitigating housing crises that disproportionately affect low- and middle-income households. Furthermore, regulatory frameworks often encourage or mandate affordability components in developments financed or managed by REITs, blending market discipline with social objectives. This interplay challenges the simplistic dichotomy of profit versus purpose, illustrating that institutional investment can serve community interests without sacrificing financial viability.

Infrastructure finance provides an additional dimension. REITs specialised in owning and operating logistics centres, data hubs, telecommunications towers, and energy infrastructure underpin the modern economy's backbone. These assets, often capital-intensive and requiring sophisticated management, are critical to economic growth and technological advancement. REITs' involvement injects stability and transparency into sectors that might otherwise suffer from underinvestment or fragmentation. The capacity of REITs to access public capital markets facilitates the mobilisation of resources at scale, thereby reducing reliance on government funding alone and accelerating development timelines. This dynamic positions REITs as vital partners in public-private collaborations essential for national competitiveness and innovation.

However, recognising REITs as public goods also invites scrutiny and ethical reflection. Critics argue that the commodification of essential services risks prioritising shareholder returns over community welfare, potentially leading to rent inflation, displacement, or under-provision in less profitable markets. These tensions underscore the necessity for robust governance frameworks, transparent disclosure, and accountability mechanisms that ensure REIT activities align with broader social objectives. Investors increasingly demand Environmental, Social, and Governance (ESG) integration within REIT strategies, signalling a market-driven push toward more responsible stewardship. The ongoing evolution of REITs into vehicles of socially conscious capital highlights the potential for harmonising financial performance with public benefit.

This expanded role of REITs has profound implications for investors. Awareness of the societal contributions of REITs reframes investment decisions, encouraging a holistic assessment that incorporates impact alongside return. For professional and individual investors alike, appreciating the public good dimension enriches portfolio strategy and fosters engagement with the underlying assets beyond mere price fluctuations. It invites consideration of how capital deployment through REITs can support sustainable urban development, resilient infrastructure, and equitable access to essential services. In turn, this awareness can influence advocacy for regulatory environments that balance investor protections with societal needs.

In sum, REITs transcend their conventional portrayal as dividend-yielding vehicles to embody instruments of collective progress. Their capacity to finance and manage physical assets that sustain communities, economies, and technological infrastructure situates them within a broader ecosystem of public utility. Recognising this dual identity challenges investors, policymakers, and industry participants to navigate the intersection of market efficiency and social responsibility with sophistication and foresight. The narrative of REITs as public goods not only deepens our understanding of their function but also elevates the discourse on the role of capital markets in shaping the built environment and societal well-being.

Chapter 11
Real Wealth Without Real Walls

Wealth, for centuries, has been inextricably linked to the tangible—the land we claim, the property we inhabit, the assets we can see and touch. Yet in an era defined by digital transformation and financial innovation, this long-held paradigm demands reconsideration. Chapter 11: *Real Wealth Without Real Walls* invites a profound rethinking of ownership, urging readers to move beyond the emotional weight of bricks and mortar and to explore the liberating possibilities offered by Real Estate Investment Trusts (REITs). Here, wealth is measured not by the walls that enclose it but by the income it generates, the flexibility it provides, and the control it confers. This chapter reframes the pursuit of prosperity, shifting the focus from possession to empowerment.

In this modern conception, ownership is no longer synonymous with a single, immovable deed. It becomes a mosaic of fractional stakes across diverse, income-producing real estate—spanning sectors, cities, and even countries. This portfolio-oriented view cultivates a sense of belonging not to a single location, but to a carefully structured financial ecosystem that balances growth, stability, and personal values. In essence, a REIT portfolio functions as a living, evolving entity: an intangible home for capital, one that adapts to ambitions, life changes, and ethical priorities. The chapter provides readers with frameworks to develop their own REIT philosophy—aligning financial decisions with lifestyle objectives and cultivating a portfolio that is simultaneously expressive and profitable.

The freedom found in releasing the compulsion for sole, physical ownership is striking. Direct property management carries heavy burdens: maintenance, illiquidity, and geographic restrictions often limit both freedom and returns. REITs, by contrast, offer scalable and diversified exposure, unshackled from these constraints. Investors gain access to ownership stakes in shopping centres, hospitals, data hubs, and city infrastructure—assets typically beyond the reach of individual capital. Though invisible in a conventional sense, these holdings exert tangible economic influence and create measurable wealth. Recognising this broadened notion of ownership transforms investment from passive participation into an active engagement with the economic and urban landscape.

Throughout the chapter, practical guidance intersects with philosophical reflection and illustrative narratives. Readers are encouraged to grapple with the tension between the tangible and the intangible, tradition and innovation, scarcity and scalability. Case studies and mental models dismantle the old assumption that wealth must be tied to physical structures, repositioning it instead as a dynamic relationship with capital—one prioritising freedom, yield, and strategic flexibility. This perspective resonates particularly with contemporary investors: digital nomads, career-fluid professionals, and value-conscious savers who seek robust financial security without the constraints of traditional property ownership.

Ultimately, *Real Wealth Without Real Walls* is a call to expand the boundaries of ownership. It asks readers to view real estate not merely as land or edifices, but as an interconnected lattice of opportunities accessible via REITs. The chapter challenges conventional notions of belonging, control, and growth, presenting wealth as an adaptable, scalable, and deeply personal construct. Each section is designed to provoke reflection, offering the intellectual and practical tools necessary to embrace asset autonomy and to cultivate a more flexible, empowered, and enduring conception of prosperity.

From Real Estate Addiction to Asset Autonomy

The traditional allure of real estate investment has long been rooted in the tangible: the solidity of brick and mortar, the psychological comfort of physical possession. This tangible ownership carries with it a profound emotional resonance—homes are not merely assets but repositories of identity, security, and legacy. Yet this deep-seated attachment can transform into an obsession, a form of *real estate addiction* that restricts flexibility, burdens capital, and ultimately narrows an investor's horizon. *From Real Estate Addiction to Asset Autonomy* invites readers to rethink this paradigm, exploring how releasing the compulsion for physical ownership can unlock genuine financial freedom—an autonomy grounded not in possession, but in yield, scalability, and strategic agility.

The psychological underpinnings of this addiction are powerful. For many, wealth is equated with the visible, the immovable. The acquisition of property signals achievement and permanence, seemingly immune to the volatility and intangibility of modern financial markets. Yet, paradoxically, this fixation often generates a form of financial fragility. Capital becomes locked in illiquid assets that require active management, significant upkeep, and exposure to local market idiosyncrasies. The emotional satisfaction derived from direct ownership is counterbalanced by the stress of tenant issues, fluctuating property values, and geographic constraints. This contradiction—between emotional security and financial rigidity—is the crucible in which the need for *asset autonomy* emerges.

Asset autonomy, as a concept, shifts the investor's focus from owning property *per se* to owning the *economic benefits* of property—cash flow, capital appreciation, and diversification—without the operational burdens. REITs and similar investment vehicles exemplify this shift, offering exposure to real estate markets while maintaining liquidity and professional management. This model dissolves the binary between tangible and intangible, transforming real estate into a flexible, scalable, and democratised asset class. Investors can now recalibrate wealth not as a physical dominion but as a dynamic portfolio engineered for income and growth, unshackled from the necessity of being 'on the ground.'

Critically, redefining wealth in terms of freedom and yield necessitates confronting entrenched cultural narratives. Societies have long valorised landownership as a status symbol and foundation of power. This reverence is reflected in tax laws, social norms, and even personal aspirations. However, the *freedom* that REITs confer—freedom from direct management, geographic tethering, and concentrated risk—offers a compelling counterpoint. It encourages investors to embrace a *portfolio identity* over a *property identity*, acknowledging that the true measure of wealth lies in the capacity to deploy capital effectively and flexibly over time.

This transition also speaks to the realities of the contemporary economy. Globalisation, demographic shifts, and technological change demand investment approaches that are agile and diversified. Direct real estate ownership often fails to keep pace with these demands, encumbered by slow transaction times and illiquidity. Conversely, asset autonomy aligns with the imperatives of modern wealth management: digital access, fractional ownership, and the integration of environmental, social, and governance (ESG) considerations. Investors who master this mindset find themselves positioned to leverage global real estate trends without sacrificing personal freedom or financial resilience.

The chapter further dissects the practical benefits of asset autonomy, illustrating how yield-driven investing can offer both income stability and growth potential. While physical property investment often focuses heavily on capital appreciation or tax advantages, REIT-based strategies prioritise consistent dividend streams supported by diversified, professionally managed portfolios. This approach mitigates the volatility and management overhead of direct ownership, allowing investors to capitalise on the underlying economic performance of a broad array of real estate assets—from commercial centres and residential complexes to data infrastructure and healthcare facilities.

However, the embrace of asset autonomy does not dismiss the psychological and philosophical dimensions of ownership; rather, it reframes them. Ownership becomes less about possession and more about participation. By holding REIT shares, investors become fractional stakeholders in the cities and communities where these assets reside. This 'invisible ownership' carries with it an ethical dimension—investors influence urban development, infrastructure provision, and social housing indirectly but meaningfully. Thus, asset autonomy offers not just financial liberation but also a new form of civic engagement.

There remain, naturally, tensions and trade-offs. The loss of direct control over physical assets challenges traditional notions of security and influence. Some investors may find the intangible nature of REIT ownership dissatisfying or feel exposed to market risks divorced from a concrete asset base. Furthermore, the complexity of

REIT structures and market dynamics requires investor education and sophistication. Yet, these challenges underscore the importance of cultivating a nuanced, informed approach rather than succumbing to emotional attachment or simplistic heuristics.

This exploration culminates in a call to reconceive wealth as a dynamic interplay between freedom, yield, and identity. By transcending real estate addiction, investors liberate themselves to craft portfolios that reflect both their financial ambitions and personal values. The shift from tangible walls to intangible yields is not merely a tactical adjustment; it represents an evolution in how wealth is conceived, accessed, and experienced.

From Real Estate Addiction to Asset Autonomy thus serves as both a practical guide and a philosophical treatise, equipping readers to navigate the emotional and economic dimensions of real estate investing in the 21st century. It challenges the reader to question inherited assumptions and to embrace a more expansive, agile, and ultimately empowering vision of wealth—one where real estate is no longer a physical possession to be hoarded, but a fluid and accessible source of enduring financial freedom.

Designing Your Personal REIT Philosophy

Designing a personal philosophy for REIT investing is not merely a matter of financial calculation; it is a deliberate, introspective process that aligns capital deployment with individual values, goals, and lifestyle choices. In an investment landscape increasingly defined by complexity and choice, this subchapter foregrounds the necessity of intentionality—a framework that transcends generic advice and situates REIT investment within the broader context of one's financial identity. *Designing Your Personal REIT Philosophy* offers more than a checklist; it is an invitation to engage in critical reflection and strategic self-definition, recognising that the most enduring investment success arises from coherence between one's inner compass and external decisions.

At the outset, it is crucial to confront a common misconception: that REITs, by virtue of their market accessibility and liquidity, require little beyond a mechanical selection process. This reductive view neglects the nuance and variability inherent in the sector—from diverse property types and geographic exposures to differing income profiles and risk tolerances. Instead, each investor must grapple with fundamental questions about their appetite for volatility, income needs, time horizons, and ethical priorities. These questions, while challenging, form the bedrock of a resilient investment philosophy, anchoring choices in a meaningful context rather than transient market trends.

To facilitate this process, mental models serve as indispensable tools. Consider the framework of *investment archetypes*: the cautious steward prioritising capital preservation and steady income; the growth-oriented architect seeking sector innovation and capital appreciation; the values-driven participant integrating ESG criteria with financial returns. Recognising which archetype resonates empowers investors to filter REIT opportunities through a lens that honours personal predilections. For instance, a cautious steward might prioritise healthcare and industrial REITs with stable tenancy, while the growth-oriented architect might allocate to data centre or technology-focused REITs. This self-awareness avoids the pitfalls of ill-fitting investment and nurtures alignment.

Reflection prompts deepen this inquiry by encouraging investors to articulate their relationship to wealth and risk. What role does real estate play in your financial life—is it a cornerstone of stability, a source of passive income, or a vehicle for aggressive growth? How do you perceive the trade-off between dividend yield and capital appreciation? What is your comfort level with market fluctuations, and how does that inform your tolerance for different REIT sectors? Such introspective questions illuminate not only strategic direction but also psychological readiness, acknowledging that investment decisions are as much about mindset as metrics.

The notion of lifestyle alignment is often overlooked but essential. REIT investing must accommodate, not constrain, an investor's lived experience. For a professional with limited time and energy, a broadly diversified REIT ETF may represent the ideal balance of exposure and simplicity. Conversely, an investor with domain expertise or sector passion might gravitate towards direct REIT selection, engaging actively with management commentary and market developments. Aligning investment approach with available resources and personal inclinations fosters sustainability, reducing the risk of disengagement or reactive behaviour in volatile markets.

Equally important is the integration of ethical reflection within the REIT philosophy. The increasing prominence of ESG factors calls for a discerning approach to sector selection and fund choice. Some investors may prioritise REITs that contribute to affordable housing, renewable energy infrastructure, or community development, while others focus on carbon footprint reduction or governance standards. This ethical overlay does not necessitate sacrificing financial returns; rather, it reframes success in terms of broader impact, forging a pathway where profit and purpose coexist. *Designing Your Personal REIT Philosophy* insists on this fusion of pragmatism and principle, underscoring that investment is ultimately an expression of values.

Conceptual tensions inevitably arise within this design process, demanding nuanced navigation. The desire for diversification may conflict with concentration in high-conviction sectors; the allure of high yield must be balanced against dividend sustainability; the promise of growth entails acceptance of volatility. Each tension represents an opportunity for deeper understanding rather than paralysis. By articulating priorities and thresholds—whether through formal decision matrices or informal mental heuristics—investors equip themselves to respond to these trade-offs with clarity and consistency.

Real-world examples enrich this discourse. Consider the contrast between an investor who adopts a REIT philosophy centred on stable, income-generating assets aligned with retirement income needs versus one who pursues a high-growth, technology infrastructure focus reflecting a longer time horizon and higher risk tolerance. Both paths are valid, reflecting divergent philosophies rather than superior or inferior strategies. Case studies of investors navigating sector rotations, market cycles, and evolving personal circumstances illustrate how philosophy is a living construct, adaptable yet anchored.

Finally, it is vital to acknowledge the meta-philosophical dimension: the process of *designing* a REIT philosophy itself cultivates discipline, patience, and self-knowledge. This process resists the temptations of herd mentality and market noise, privileging deliberate, values-based decision-making. It aligns investment not merely with financial outcomes but with a coherent life narrative, transforming portfolio management into a practice of intentional stewardship.

In sum, *Designing Your Personal REIT Philosophy* is an essential exercise in self-mastery and strategic clarity. It challenges readers to move beyond transactional approaches, fostering a robust, authentic investment identity. Through critical reflection, mental modelling, and ethical engagement, investors gain the tools to construct a REIT portfolio that is not only financially sound but deeply resonant with their unique life and goals. This alignment—between who you are, what you value, and how you invest—ultimately shapes the trajectory of wealth as a source of both security and meaning.

The Portfolio as a Place of Belonging

A portfolio, much like a home, is more than a mere structure—it is a repository of identity, a sanctuary of stability, and a foundation for growth. The parallels between traditional homes and modern investment portfolios reveal profound truths about how we seek security and belonging in our financial lives. In an era where physical ownership is no longer the sole marker of wealth or comfort, understanding the portfolio as a place of belonging challenges investors to reconsider what it means to possess value, to anchor oneself, and to nurture future prosperity. This reflection transcends simplistic notions of asset allocation and ventures into the territory where finance intersects with psychology, culture, and purpose.

The concept of 'home' carries an almost archetypal weight in human experience—evoking safety, permanence, and personal narrative. Yet, the realities of contemporary life increasingly complicate this ideal. High housing costs, geographic mobility, and shifting generational preferences have diluted the traditional equation of wealth with physical real estate ownership. *Financial portfolios, particularly those centred on real estate investment trusts (REITs), offer a new paradigm: ownership without walls, stability without immobility.* Here, investors may hold diversified claims in tangible assets spanning malls, offices, hospitals, and data centres—properties that, while intangible in everyday perception, are integral to the economy and society.

This shift invites a re-examination of stability. While a home's stability is physical and spatial, a portfolio's stability is temporal and structural. It derives from diversification across sectors, geographies, and investment vehicles, mitigating idiosyncratic risk and cushioning against market volatility. For instance, a REIT portfolio combining healthcare facilities with logistics centres and residential complexes can offer a more resilient income stream than any single property investment. This dynamic stability functions much like a well-constructed home: capable of weathering external shocks while providing continuous shelter. The investor's psychological comfort, often underestimated, is enhanced by this architectural financial design.

Identity within a portfolio manifests through the deliberate selection and weighting of assets, reflecting the investor's values, goals, and risk appetite. Much as a homeowner might personalise their living space to express taste and heritage, an investor curates holdings to express beliefs—be it commitment to sustainable development through green REITs, engagement with urban revitalisation via community-focused properties, or pursuit of innovative sectors like data infrastructure. These choices signal not only financial intent but also an ethical and philosophical stance. *The portfolio becomes a mirror and extension of self,* offering a sense of belonging to larger economic and social narratives.

Growth, the third pillar of this triad, encapsulates both capital appreciation and income generation. Just as a home's value may increase through renovation or neighbourhood development, a portfolio's worth grows through strategic rebalancing, reinvestment of dividends, and harnessing economic trends. The concept of compounding income in REITs, where dividends are reinvested to purchase additional shares, creates a self-sustaining growth engine. Importantly, this growth is not divorced from stability or identity; it is the fruit of conscious stewardship. Investors who see their portfolios as living entities, evolving with their circumstances and broader market dynamics, are more likely to navigate volatility with equanimity and foresight.

Yet, the metaphorical comparison invites critical reflection. Unlike a home—an inherently private and singular space—a portfolio is inherently interconnected with global markets, regulatory frameworks, and collective investor behaviour. This interdependence means that belonging in a financial sense also entails exposure to systemic risks and ethical considerations. The challenge lies in balancing personal agency with the realities of these external forces, fostering a portfolio that is both personally meaningful and pragmatically resilient.

Real-world applications underscore this philosophy. Consider the investor who diversifies their REIT holdings across stable core assets for income, alongside opportunistic growth REITs in emerging markets. This blend echoes the notion of a home with both a secure foundation and adaptive, innovative spaces—spaces that reflect the fluidity of life and ambition. Similarly, institutional investors increasingly integrate ESG criteria, weaving social responsibility into the fabric of their portfolios, thus redefining belonging not only as individual security but as communal stewardship.

Moreover, the digital age has expanded the portfolio's reach as a place of belonging. Online platforms and fractional investing democratise access to diverse REITs, allowing investors to construct personalised portfolios that might have been infeasible previously. This accessibility amplifies the psychological and practical dimensions of belonging, enabling investors to feel connected to global real estate markets and the economic ecosystems they support.

This synthesis of stability, identity, and growth positions the portfolio not as a cold aggregation of assets, but as a dynamic place—an evolving home for wealth and values. It challenges the investor to engage with their portfolio beyond mere performance metrics, fostering a deeper relationship characterised by reflection, intentionality, and stewardship.

Ultimately, embracing the portfolio as a place of belonging reorients investment from a transactional endeavour to a holistic practice. It honours the emotional and existential dimensions of wealth, recognising that financial structures—when thoughtfully designed—can provide not only economic returns but also a profound sense of rootedness and purpose. This paradigm invites investors to craft portfolios that resonate with their life's narrative, transforming abstract capital into tangible, lived experience.

You Own More Than You Think

To own a Real Estate Investment Trust (REIT) share is, in essence, to hold a fractional stake in a sprawling, often unseen portfolio of tangible assets—malls bustling with consumers, hospitals providing critical care, data centres powering the digital economy, and urban infrastructure shaping the contours of modern cities. This ownership transcends the physical confines of property; it embodies a complex web of economic, social, and technological realities, often invisible to the individual investor but palpably real in impact. The paradox lies in how this invisible ownership manifests tangible value and influence in everyday life, positioning the REIT shareholder not merely as a distant financier but as a steward of essential societal functions.

The allure of REITs traditionally lies in their capacity to deliver stable income streams and portfolio diversification. Yet beneath these financial metrics exists a profound narrative: through REIT ownership, investors become silent partners in the infrastructures that define contemporary civilisation. Consider, for instance, the retail REITs that own and manage shopping centres, which serve as vital community hubs—not only places of commerce but social gathering points fostering economic vitality. Similarly, healthcare REITs underpin the delivery of medical services by investing in hospital facilities, senior living communities, and specialised clinics. These assets, often taken for granted, are pivotal in sustaining public health and social welfare.

Investors in data centre REITs, though less visible, are at the forefront of the digital transformation, funding the facilities that store and process the vast torrents of information defining our connected lives. This includes everything from streaming media to cloud computing services integral to businesses and individuals alike. The significance of this ownership extends beyond capital appreciation and dividends; it embodies participation in the infrastructure enabling the 21st-century economy.

A deeper understanding of this ownership emerges when one acknowledges the layered complexity of REIT structures. Unlike direct real estate investment, REITs provide a vehicle for fractionalised and professional management of diverse property portfolios. This pooling of capital allows individuals to access scale and expertise typically reserved for institutional players. It also imposes regulatory frameworks that ensure transparency and protect investors, reinforcing the integrity of their participation in these asset ecosystems.

Yet, the 'invisibility' of ownership can sometimes obscure the real-world implications. For many investors, the connection between holding REIT shares and owning part of a hospital or data centre remains abstract. This distance may foster a limited appreciation of the social responsibilities and risks inherent in real estate investment. For example, the performance of REITs can be affected by shifts in regulatory policies, urban development trends, or technological disruptions, each with cascading effects on communities and economies. Understanding this interdependence is essential for investors aiming to align their portfolios with both financial goals and broader societal impact.

This recognition also raises ethical considerations. REIT investors, by virtue of their ownership, indirectly influence property management decisions, development priorities, and even urban planning. For example, choices about sustainability initiatives, affordable housing projects, or digital infrastructure investments reflect values that resonate beyond balance sheets. Some investors actively seek REITs committed to environmental, social, and governance (ESG) principles, recognising that their capital can catalyse positive change. Others may grapple with the tension between profit maximisation and social responsibility, highlighting the nuanced role of REIT ownership in shaping communities.

Real-world case studies illuminate these dynamics. Public Storage, a REIT specialising in self-storage facilities, has benefited from demographic shifts and lifestyle changes, reflecting how seemingly mundane assets adapt to evolving social patterns. Prologis, a global logistics REIT, plays a critical role in supply chain infrastructure, especially evident during periods of economic disruption like the COVID-19 pandemic. Healthcare REITs such as Ventas and Healthpeak Properties provide essential capital for medical facilities, underscoring their role in public health resilience. These examples illustrate that REIT shareholders are intertwined with sectors fundamental to economic and social continuity.

Furthermore, REIT ownership offers unique opportunities for diversification that traditional real estate investing cannot match. By holding shares in multiple REITs across different sectors and geographies, investors mitigate risk and capture varied economic cycles. This broad ownership not only enhances portfolio resilience but also deepens the investor's connection to multiple facets of real estate—urban and suburban, commercial and residential, emerging technologies and established industries.

Technological advancements have further democratized this ownership, enabling retail investors to access REITs through online platforms, mutual funds, and exchange-traded funds (ETFs). This accessibility expands the investor base and fosters greater awareness of the underlying assets. However, it also requires vigilance and education to comprehend the complexities masked by market liquidity and apparent simplicity. Investors must engage with the substantive realities behind the shares they hold to fully appreciate the breadth of their ownership.

The expanding scope of REIT ownership invites a redefinition of wealth—one that transcends mere financial accumulation and encompasses participation in the built environment that sustains societal functioning. This shift aligns with contemporary calls for more conscious investing, where capital is understood not just as a means to individual gain but as a vehicle of collective consequence.

In this light, owning REITs is a form of stewardship. It confers both privilege and responsibility. Investors, as partial owners of critical infrastructure and real estate, influence the direction of economic development and community well-being, albeit indirectly. This realization empowers shareholders to approach their investments with a broader perspective, integrating financial aspirations with civic awareness.

Ultimately, the paradox of REIT ownership—being both invisible and profoundly real—invites a richer narrative about investment. It challenges investors to look beyond stock prices and dividends to the societal and economic ecosystems they support. By recognising the tangible footprint of their ownership, investors can cultivate a sense of belonging and purpose within the vast and interconnected domain of real estate. This awareness transforms passive holding into active engagement, fostering portfolios that reflect not only personal ambition but also a commitment to the shared spaces that shape our collective future.

Conclusion

Ownership, long synonymous with tangible markers—a key in the hand, a fenced plot, a deed inscribed on paper—has undergone a profound transformation. In today's landscape, authority does not stem from walls or land alone but from the mastery of structure, clarity, and the courage to navigate intricate financial frameworks. This shift mirrors a broader economic and cultural evolution: ownership has become a dynamic, system-driven engagement rather than a mere accumulation of assets. The book closes not with a perfunctory summary, but with an invitation to inhabit this new paradigm: recognising that the most astute investors no longer aspire simply to reside in homes, but to hold stakes in the very frameworks—commercial, residential, infrastructural—that shape the world.

Such a conceptual evolution demands a redefinition of real estate ownership in the twenty-first century. The classic image of property as a discrete, static asset has grown increasingly inadequate. Today, ownership manifests through collective structures—Real Estate Investment Trusts (REITs), mutual funds, and other pooled vehicles—offering fractional stakes in professionally managed, income-generating assets. These instruments dismantle conventional barriers—huge capital thresholds, managerial burdens, illiquidity—while democratising access to markets once reserved for institutional actors. Yet, the shift requires more than financial literacy; it demands an investor mindset shaped by discipline, transparency, and a willingness to engage with risk in new, sometimes abstract, forms.

The modern investor navigates a terrain defined less by possession than by access. Wealth is no longer the exclusive domain of individual parcels of land or buildings; it is the ability to deploy capital across fluid portfolios spanning geographies, sectors, and regulatory environments. This flexibility opens remarkable opportunities but simultaneously challenges long-standing assumptions. How does one quantify ownership when lines between individual and institutional assets blur? What constitutes control when decisions reside with governance structures rather than personal hands? These questions underline the necessity of a strategic framework grounded in the legal, fiscal, and operational foundations of contemporary real estate investing.

Importantly, the tools for meaningful participation are within reach of the individual investor. Across preceding chapters, examples have illustrated the diversity and impact of modern REIT investment: from healthcare REITs funding hospitals to technology infrastructure trusts powering data centres. Yet this is not an argument for passive engagement; modern ownership is participatory, requiring ongoing attention to market dynamics, regulatory shifts, and evolving societal needs.

This redefinition also carries an ethical dimension often absent from traditional property ownership. Investors become stakeholders not merely in financial outcomes but in social ecosystems—affordable housing, sustainable urban planning, essential service provision. REITs and similar vehicles can channel capital towards public benefit, marking a departure from pure profit-maximisation. Here, ownership intertwines financial objectives with communal impact, adding complexity yet enriching the very meaning of investment.

Embracing this paradigm requires courage—intellectual and emotional. Intellectual, because it involves mastering law, finance, and economics; emotional, because it challenges deep-seated attachments to tangible property. Investors must reconcile the invisibility of fractional ownership with the real influence it confers, cultivating confidence not from naïve optimism but from disciplined analysis, critical judgment, and a structured approach to risk.

The assertion that "you don't just own homes—you own the systems that house the world" encapsulates this evolution. Ownership is increasingly about integration—into networks of assets, markets, and communities that collectively define the built environment. Recognising this connection transforms portfolios from static holdings into dynamic entities that actively contribute to the fabric of modern life.

The book's final chapters have provided a roadmap for understanding, evaluating, and engaging with these systems. They empower readers to move from passive observation to informed participation. The challenge ahead is continuous: to question, adapt, and refine strategies as the landscape shifts.

Ultimately, this new model of ownership confers freedom—not merely freedom from physical constraints, but the freedom to harness complexity for intentional investment. It is the ability to exercise control through clarity, to participate through connection, and to build wealth through thoughtful engagement rather than mere accumulation. This represents the frontier of contemporary real estate investing—and the opportunity awaiting those ready to embrace it.

A Different Kind of Ownership

Ownership is no longer what it once was. The traditional markers—keys that open a front door, fences encircling a parcel of land, deeds recorded in government offices—once symbolised control and permanence. Today, these tangible symbols have ceded their primacy to a more nuanced, complex concept: ownership defined by clarity, structure, and above all, courage. This shift reflects a profound transformation in how wealth and property intertwine, driven by technological advances, financial innovation, and evolving societal norms. In this changing landscape, the smartest investors will not merely live within homes; they will own the systems that shape where and how we live, work, and connect. This is an invitation to grasp that broader form of ownership and the freedoms it unlocks.

The impetus behind this transformation stems from the growing realisation that *accumulating physical assets*—while comforting in its familiarity—is often inefficient, inaccessible, and inflexible. Ownership has expanded beyond individual, discrete properties to encompass fractional interests in portfolios that span cities, sectors, and even continents. Real Estate Investment Trusts (REITs), mutual funds, and exchange-traded funds (ETFs) illustrate this evolution, offering investors entry points to vast real estate ecosystems without the burdens of direct property management. Such vehicles harness economies of scale, professional expertise, and market liquidity, making real estate ownership a dynamic, scalable experience. Yet, these benefits come with demands: clarity to understand complex structures, the discipline to navigate risks, and the courage to participate actively rather than cling to outdated notions of possession.

This broader ownership demands an investor's mindset tuned to the architecture of modern markets. Instead of physical keys, the investor wields knowledge of legal frameworks, tax implications, and market dynamics. Ownership becomes a responsibility, not only for personal gain but also for stewardship—supporting developments in infrastructure, affordable housing, and sustainable urban environments. These responsibilities align investment with social purpose, redefining wealth as a force that shapes communities and economies rather than a mere accumulation of assets. Investors who recognise this interdependence are positioned to harness both financial and societal returns, understanding that their portfolios are intertwined with the fabric of contemporary life.

Real-world examples vividly illustrate this shift. Consider a REIT focusing on data centres—these digital fortresses underpin cloud computing, global communications, and the burgeoning digital economy. By investing in such an entity, an individual becomes a silent partner in an infrastructure critical to modern civilisation, yet without ever touching a physical server or property deed. Similarly, healthcare REITs finance hospitals and senior living facilities, tangibly impacting public health outcomes. These investments embody the invisible nature of modern ownership: *intangible, dispersed, yet profoundly real and consequential.* The power of this ownership lies precisely in its system-wide reach and professional stewardship, offering a kind of influence that transcends traditional property boundaries.

However, this new form of ownership requires *courage*—the courage to depart from the security of bricks and mortar and embrace complexity and abstraction. Investors must resist the allure of simplistic narratives that equate wealth with tangible possession alone. Instead, they must develop sophistication to evaluate structures, governance, and long-term sustainability. This courage is not reckless but informed and disciplined, recognising that clarity in understanding fuels confidence, while ignorance fosters vulnerability. Investors who engage actively with the systems they own—through due diligence, ongoing education, and strategic patience—are those who thrive.

At its core, this evolution challenges entrenched ideas about wealth and freedom. Physical ownership once promised control, but often it shackled capital and constrained opportunity. Today, ownership defined by access to systems and markets offers liquidity, diversification, and the ability to respond nimbly to change. This shift democratizes real estate investment, enabling broader participation across socioeconomic lines. It repositions wealth as a networked concept, where ownership is shared, managed, and perpetually reconfigured. Far from diminishing control, this model offers a *different kind of autonomy*—one grounded in insight, adaptability, and engagement.

The implications extend beyond finance. As ownership detaches from physical form, it aligns with broader cultural trends towards access economy models and digital transformation. People prioritise experiences and flexibility over permanence, and investments must mirror these values. REITs and similar instruments reflect this zeitgeist by enabling fluid, participatory ownership that is responsive to contemporary lifestyles and goals. They redefine what it means to "own" real estate, not by the solidity of walls but by the resilience of income streams, governance quality, and alignment with personal values.

Ultimately, to own the systems that house the world is to participate in a collective endeavour—one that shapes the environments in which societies grow and thrive. This ownership is neither abstract nor passive; it is a conscious, strategic stance that demands clarity to understand complexity, structure to navigate uncertainty, and courage to seize opportunity. The invitation offered here is not merely to invest, but to belong—to the networks of capital and community that define modern real estate and, by extension, modern life.

This transformative conception of ownership is the defining theme of contemporary real estate investment. It invites readers to reconsider their relationship with property, wealth, and freedom. It challenges assumptions and encourages a deliberate, informed approach to participation in these vast, interconnected systems. As this book has shown, the keys of the future are intangible but potent—knowledge, discipline, and courage. With these, investors are equipped not just to own homes, but to own the frameworks that sustain and enrich the world we inhabit.

About the Author

Adrian Lorne writes at the intersection of modern finance, behavioral psychology, and personal freedom. With a passion for turning complexity into clarity, his work empowers readers to think differently about ownership, wealth, and the systems that govern them. Adrian's background spans global markets, minimalist living, and a decade-long inquiry into how ordinary people can build extraordinary portfolios—without sacrificing flexibility or peace of mind. He believes real estate is no longer bound by physical walls, and his writing shows readers how to own powerfully in an age of detachment and design.

www.ingramcontent.com/pod-product-compliance
Lightning Source LLC
Chambersburg PA
CBHW031349230926
51848CB00002B/452
9789371776929